Fear Itself

Fear Itself

CANDIDA LAWRENCE

UNBRIDLED
BOOKS
2004

UNBRIDLED BOOKS,
Denver, Colorado

Library of Congress Cataloging-in-Publication Data

Lawrence, Candida
Fear Itself / Candida Lawrence.
p. cm.
ISBN 1-932961-01-1
1. Lawrence, Candida—Health.   2. Radiation
injuries—Patients—United States—Biography.
I. Title.
RC93.L39 2004
362.196'9897'0092—DC22
2004016269

1   3   5   7   9   10   8   6   4   2

Book Design by SH · CV

ACKNOWLEDGMENTS

On my first day of school, I encountered the Pledge of Allegiance. At dinner I asked: "What's a pledge?" My father said, "A pledge is a promise."

"What's leegence?" He wasn't quick to answer, and I moved on, "What's a republic?"

"It's a country whose citizens vote to choose who will lead them. . . . I suppose your next question is 'indivisible'?" Yeah, I said. Yes, said my mother, not yeah. "Liberty and justice I'll explain tomorrow," he said. "I have a headache. Tonight I just want to say that you do not have to recite the pledge when the teacher tells you to, or ever."

"But I have to; everyone has to."

He looked pained, "No, you don't have to, because you cannot promise to respect a country today when it might not behave well next month, or tomorrow. Understand?"

I acknowledge his early influence on a child already not much inclined to follow rules. I wish he were alive to tangle with me today on which windmills to challenge. He died in 1981.

Special thanks to Fred Ramey, always kind, patient, faithful and clever, and to Kathy Chetkovich who has read most that I've written and has found something to praise even in weak efforts.

To John Sperling I offer the small voice of gratitude for being the Tabasco Sauce in my life.

Be mindful, when invention fails,
To scratch your head, and bite your nails.

—JONATHAN SWIFT

There is occasions and causes why and
Wherefore in all things.

—SHAKEPEARE, *HENRY V*

1932

BERKELEY, CALIFORNIA

I'm sitting high up in a eucalyptus tree with a yo-yo in my left hand. There's a breeze and the leaves are squeaking. The smell is my favorite, better even than horses or kittens. The tree is in a sloped vacant lot next to my house, and the grass below me is flat where I've been sliding down on a piece of cardboard. My mother is probably in the kitchen I can see from my perch, and she's no doubt washing my baby brother on a canvas table set up next to the sink. He's okay, but he cries a lot and gets me thinking about things. He must be breakable because my mother never takes her eyes or hands off him. You'd think no baby had ever been born that lived on to walk and talk. Since his arrival she spends less time wondering where I am and what I'm doing, and that's fine by me. I guess you might say I'm hiding, something I do a lot these days. My sister is with my mother, helping with a diaper or cooing or powdering. She's two years older than I am, which makes her ten and me eight. It's Saturday, which is why we aren't in school.

Lately I've been asking myself where things come from. I don't mean my brother. I know what they say—sperm, egg, womb, getting born—and I've seen the male cat get on top of our Kit-Kat and later the kittens come out in their sacs and I suppose it was like that with Daddy and Molly (my mother changed her name from Violette to Molly in college and has always preferred our saying Molly instead of Mommy). All that sperm and egg stuff just seems natural, like grass growing and tulips pushing up in the front garden, birds nesting, laying eggs, feeding the open beaks. What puzzles me is the yo-yo in my hand—and other *things,* like my skates at the base of the tree and the skate key around my neck. Marbles. My jacks and the red ball.

Here's how I get to the puzzlement. I'm sitting in

this tree and I think to myself, I'm a little girl sitting in a tree with a yo-yo in my hand and I'm feeling alone and happy, and then I start wondering if I'm the only little girl in the world sitting in a tree and I'm sure I'm not. I start trying to figure how many of us there are at this moment in the world and I travel in my mind to China, Australia, everywhere I can think of and imagine just oodles of girls in trees. Then I think of all the fathers and mothers and sisters and baby brothers and the houses and kitchens and skates and yo-yos. The world is just crawling with boys and girls and parents and for a moment I'm above the world looking down at all these busy ant-people going in and out of houses, fixing food, washing babies, making babies. I tell you it's quite a thought to have up a tree and the only place all this occurs to me is right there.

What I can't stop thinking about is not the numbers—I know I can't really imagine how many—it's what all these people are making, like yo-yos. Skates. I start with the yo-yo because it seems simple and I carry mine everywhere I go. I'm a great yo-yo player. Mine's made of wood and has a crack where the string goes and is attached with a staple. The wood is half-yellow, half-red on both sides, and when it spins it looks orange. Some of this is easy. The wood comes from a tree and the crack is carved with a knife. Here's where it gets hard. The knife, the staple, the string, the turning orange. Knives are made of steel, but where does the steel come from? The string? Cotton is a plant, but how does it become string? The staple is probably steel too, but how does it turn into a staple? Who thought up string? Who invented a yo-yo?

My mind doesn't spend much time snagged on these silly questions. I *know* I can climb down from the tree and go ask my smart parents for answers. We have the *Book of Knowledge* and Daddy is a jittery encyclopedia. They just love for their children to ask questions. They glow when they answer. It's the next stage that I keep a secret, the part where I'm wondering if human beings just can't help making things— automobiles, can openers, telephones, refrigerators, books, eyeglasses (which I wear), batteries—oh, I could go on and on. And why is it that animals don't, and did it just happen that way or is it a big Plan put in motion somehow by Somebody? I don't let anyone know I'm having these thoughts. I don't want to be interrupted. It's delicious to wonder. If they knew, my parents would worry. The truth is that the Somebody idea is like eating a whole tablespoon of hard sauce. (Who invented hard sauce?) It tastes so good but seems to scald the inside of my head, and afterwards I wish I'd eaten an apple instead.

1935

ECHO LAKE, THE SIERRAS

I'm sitting on a large, flat, warm slab of granite high above our mountain cabin. Nearby is Saucer Lake, and far below me is Echo Lake and cabins and kids and parents and outhouses. I can see the lake, the shape curiously unfamiliar, and the motorboats looking like skeeters on the water. I'm not supposed to be up here alone because the adults have rules about hiking. You always have to go with someone, wear a hat, not eat much before or during, drink water sparingly, and chew gum—I forget why. Molly thinks I'm resting in my tent. It's a rule that you rest after lunch. Another rule is that you can't go swimming alone and not until two hours after eating. All I want to do is practice my swan dive, but I wouldn't be doing that today anyway because another rule is that you can't swim when you have the curse, which I have.

Yesterday was my first day and all of a sudden Molly told me about bleeding every month until I'm old and about sanitary napkins and belts to hold them up and how to dispose of the soiled napkins (wrap them in toilet paper, throw them down the hole in the outhouse, pour lime over them). It seems that my sister has been doing this every month and I never noticed, and it just occurred to me that Molly must do it too. So now there are three of us in our little cabin who bleed and it's embarrassing for me that I can't go swimming for *four* days. Everyone knows I'm devoting my summer to diving and now they'll know I'm bleeding. The boys will know.

It's peaceful up here but I'm twitching and trembling and I'm thinking I don't want it to be a secret. I think it would be a good idea if we all just dribbled blood all over the pine-needle ground and the rocks, spilled the redness into the black waters I dive into. Molly asked me if there were any questions I wanted to ask but I couldn't think of any. She patted my shoulder and left me alone in the outhouse with the "equipment."

I lie flat on the warm rock and stare at the few clouds moving slowly across the sky. I wonder how many other girls are on their second day of bleeding and have gone off alone to think about it. This minute, this day, in the desert, in a Paris apartment, in African fields of grass? Did Meg, Amy, Jo and Beth have equipment? No, Molly said she used rags and had to wash them out and it was disgusting. Even so, there's a population out there thinking thoughts much like mine, I'm sure of it. I wonder if they have to rest after lunch, or even if they have lunch, and can they fix an outboard motor the way I can? I can take the carburetor apart and clean it, fix a cotter pin, get the ratio of gas and oil just right, to say nothing of whizzing through the low-water channel without hitting a single rock.

And now suddenly I'm thinking about the ideas in an outboard motor—the propeller, the gas engine, the rope coiled around the wheel to start it, and I know I could never invent something like that. I can fix it when it's broken but I don't understand it any more than I understand why the flashlight I use under the covers at night lights up when you push up the switch, or why the batteries have to go this way and not that way. Last semester I read a whole book on electricity and I could see that if you knew something you might be able to control its power, but still it seemed they were using words like "current" instead of just admitting it was magic, mysterious stuff.

When you think of it, it's both amazing and discouraging. People, mostly men, are sending talk via telephone across continents, flying everywhere, making radios, looking through lenses at a bacillus that causes TB, designing "equipment" for me, then making up the language that explains it all. And I'm imagining them in all their suits, in their buildings, with their tables and chairs and telephones, in their factories with noisy machinery producing more machinery and tiny parts just the right size and shape. I *know* I could never take part in all this rampaging invention. Two summers ago Daddy built a whole bedroom onto the cabin and I helped him. He built me my own tool chest with my name etched on top in copper nail-heads. I did what he told me to do. I pounded a nail where he said to and fastened hundreds of shingles. But I wondered every day how he knew what to do each moment. I mean he's a newspaper columnist and yet seemed to know what would hold up what and why. Me, I might have started with the roof, built it on the ground and raised it somehow later.

People tell me I'm smart. I get As in school. But I know there's buzzing, brilliant thought inside human beings, and all over the world people are learning things while I lie on this rock. Somehow I'm not part of it. The most I can do is think about it, wonder if we are all alone in the universe inventing and trying to understand. If we are alone and what Daddy says is true, that there's no God directing us, then it seems so brave to be making roads, accordions, cotter pins, buttons, zippers, jeans with pockets, tennies, sanitary napkins and belts with a metal doohickey to hold them up, and at least five different brands of underarm deodorant. Chewing gum.

I sit up and take my green package of spearmint gum out of my jeans pocket with the brass rivets (why?) and stare at it. There's an outer wrap and inside are five pieces of gum, each wrapped in green paper with lettering on it, and inside is the gum enfolded in tinfoil. This gum has come to me by boat (the delivery boy is real cute) from the store at the end of the lake. Molly writes an order each day and the next day he delivers everything in person. He has to carry the grocery box up the hill to our cabin. In Berkeley, I can buy spearmint lots of places, and once I asked a visitor to the house if you could buy this same gum in Paris. Yep. This inventing, packaging, selling, traveling of gum is much more amazing to me than the occasional fossil lizard print I find in granite up here above the cabin. The lizard doesn't have a clue about becoming a fossil, but some human mind wants to be able to get spearmint to my mountain cabin in the summertime. I mean, this all started in one person's head. He (it's surely a man) knew that people like to chew, and he invented a substance that wouldn't stick to your teeth or poison you if you swallowed it; then another person made a machine that formed it into thin rectangular shapes and wrapped paper around them; then someone else figured out how to roll it, fly it, float it all over the world into stores and homes. Amazing.

All these thoughts about people (men) all over the world inventing and manufacturing and selling are giving me a headache and I lie down again. I feel there should be Someone in control, to guide all this busy-ness, and it seems mighty strange that we're all alone in the universe, the only creatures inventing gum, and it's all an *accident,* as Daddy has said. He's cheerful about the idea of accident. But sometimes he gets gloomy and tells me that human beings also thought up property and God and nations and invented weapons to kill each other when they fight about these things. He was an ambulance driver in the First World War but he doesn't like to talk about it. Molly says he picked up bloody arms and legs and bodies for two years and was gassed. Someone invented gas.

I know I'll never invent anything, and if that's so, what am I going to do with the rest of my life? Especially the times of leak and wearing equipment.

It's August 15, 1945, and my husband and I are sitting on a parched Berkeley hillside staring out at the fog smearing in from the bay. Only last week I liked to say "my husband," pack a lunch into his black lunch box and make love with him on the weekend. But today I think "The man is crying" and I'm tired of comforting him.

He began crying on August 9, the day we dropped the bomb on Nagasaki, and his lovely blue eyes have been shot with blood ever since. I want very much to speak my mind but know I won't. I'm wife and woman and I'm supposed to comfort, not deliver moral lectures or various versions of I-told-you-so. I myself haven't cried since my beloved cousin was killed in an Army Air Corps training accident early in the war.

This man sitting beside me is crumpled, his thin back bent over his knees; he needs a shave, and I fear the form his recovery will take. He will say soon, perhaps this afternoon, that he really had no choice. He had to go off every day and make plutonium because, although he's only twenty-one, he was a junior physicist and the country was at war; the army wouldn't take him because he could make plutonium. The government, in fact, would not *let* him enlist, because what if he were captured and tortured and forced to tell his scientific secrets? And now that the war's over, the army will insist that he put on a uniform for a year because it feels guilty that he was allowed to pursue a normal life of marriage, lunch box, job making plutonium, while other boys had to leave home and risk their lives.

I have all the information that might lead me into comforting him, but I want instead to stand up and walk away, make myself separate. His hands tremble. He grabs an oak leaf and crumbles it. Black hairs curl around his white fingers. His blue eyes look up at me

and they seem to stutter. He tries to focus on my san-
dal, which frets and pokes at dry grass. He shudders.

"I was doing compartmentalized work. I didn't
know I was making a bomb, didn't even know I was
making plutonium. I had no idea why I was exempt
from the Army. Why a second bomb, why didn't
they stop at one, why didn't they just threaten, why?
Why?"

His eyes fill. I have no patience, scant sympathy. I
don't know why I'm so cold. I want him to stand up
and say "Back off, government! I'll do as I wish from
now on. Send me to jail, but I will not give you more
of my life." I want him to form a fist and shake it at
the sky.

He will not. He will cry—and do as he's told. I
don't want to make love with him on Saturday night,
or go with him when he leaves for Los Alamos or Oak
Ridge. I don't want to be with physicists. Most of
them are eldest or only sons who are thin, get colds
easily, and have mothers like my mother-in-law. She's
afraid he'll die if he gets his feet wet.

Now he's lying down under an oak tree, his fore-
arm covering his eyes. He doesn't want to look at me.

If I lie beside him, that's comfort. No, I'll remain sitting up and think about men making things and women comforting and, for the twentieth time since Nagasaki, wonder if our separate activities are in our genes.

And it's while fog is bringing the scent of eucalyptus to my sinuses and the birds are settling in the branches and the furry sun is slowly sinking into the bay that I begin to feel pompous, foolish, ignorant—a common female scold. Like my mother. Don't smoke, don't eat unwashed fruit, you're coughing because, you're sick because. Then, though the late afternoon is still warm, I feel chilled. We—the calibrators and comforters—we *all* made the bomb. Our friends and enemies have worked steadily to create, to discover. The Germans, the English, the Russians, the Americans, the Japanese. He made it, I made it. My ancestors. My descendants will develop something worse. We have to know. We cannot decline. There are those who believe in a God and that their God is good. Could there be a God who has planned our destruction, who knew our end when we used the first tool, the first fire?

"Let's go home," he says. "Let's not eat. Let's go to bed." He's standing above me, holding out his hand. We are twenty-one and twenty, married. I think of candlelight, of skin, mine tanned and smooth, his white and tender, our skins touching—not burned, not scorched or peeling. We shall ride home in our ancient maroon Packard convertible with the chrome Winged Victory leading the way. We will not utter another word until morning.

1945

OAK RIDGE, TENNESSEE

We trade in the Packard for a practical, larger Oldsmobile, light green. On army orders, we go to Los Alamos National Laboratory for two weeks. No married couple housing, sour people urging us east, ordering us, forms to fill out. We drive on to Oak Ridge, Tennessee. I read *The Grand Inquisitor* to my husband when he is at the wheel. I want him to understand it. He says it is a good story, the Russian can really get fired up, can't he? I say there's more, don't you see? More? Tell me. But I can't. He should know without asking. There's something annoyingly dim-bulby about him, a flickering light, as though he's saving electricity. Is he just a simple soul, as my father says, a good boy, as my mother insists, someone I am safe with? Why is it that when he puts on a Pfc uniform, he looks diminished, thinner, sickly? He is wearing his summer issue uniform, and the beige monotone seems to have leached blue from his eyes, turning them a feeble gray. At gas stations he comes alive as he checks the tires, the oil, the carburetor, while I wonder if I can hitch a ride back to the coast with any driver headed in that direction. If he were a different kind of man, not so "good," I could tell him that and he would laugh. I could even leave him, say "Bye, husband. I want my story to begin." I want to be Jo but feel like Beth.

Oak Ridge. Six weeks. A place of gates, guards in uniform, fences, barracks, flatness in all directions. Hot. Army ID gets us in. Special permission gets us out only once—to Knoxville for dinner. We are prisoners, and I feel that is just punishment. My husband mutely disappears into his "work." He is not free to say what that is. I am well trained and do not pry.

We live in a dormitory barracks, makeshift quarters for married couples. We sleep in our private bed-

room, eat in a cafeteria, wash clothes in a laundry tub
in the basement, hang wet clothes on a communal
line. My trousseau begins to disappear. Also just, it
seems to me. Our allotment is insufficient, and I get a
job at the government employment agency, an aluminum cube. The applicants have no addresses, no
last names, are black, won't look at me. The facilities and water fountains outside the door are labeled:
White. Black. I feel my name fading, my identity stuck
to paper that might blow away. Cretins, I think. All of
us. Brotherhood? When was that? Who said it? Sister,
I think, but do not murmur. I push her job assignment towards her, tell her to go to Building 3E tomorrow morning.

In the evening that never seems to grow dark, I
follow him in the cafeteria line, say again and again
"Did you know that . . . ?" but can't hear his answer in
the heat, the noise of crashing dishes. The sweat from
black brows drips into the plates offered to us, the
food left untouched on sticky tables. I crave raw fruit
and vegetables, lose weight, drink whites-only water,
feel myself vanishing inside state power. Though our

portion of Oak Ridge is small, it is clear that taxes have gone to produce a city—area, massive buildings, thousands of employees. No one has planted a garden, created a park, set up a newsstand. There is dusty, cracked clay, but no earth.

My next job is in the town's only bank, a bungalow with low ceilings and a guard with a gun at the front door. Our boss is a thin man in his midthirties who hovers over his all-female staff. He darts into his small office, bends over papers on his desk, comes out again, drinks water from our bottled water dispenser, teases his "girls," worries over bounced checks, comments on what we are wearing. We are all tellers and Monday through Thursday we do next to nothing. Friday is pay day and the cages are open from 7:00 A.M. to 7:00 P.M. Our hands turn grimy with ink and dirt as we push money across the counter into black hands, white hands, seldom looking up, dripping with sweat. We eat our hamburgers and down our cokes while we pay and count and stack coins.

My co-workers wear one-piece bathing suits—black, pink, striped, often with a teasing ruffle around the hips. I am amazed at the bathing suits and refuse to retrieve my two-piece Hawaiian cotton number from the bottom of my suitcase. I wear a pink sundress with a white bolero day after day, sometimes still wet from a washing the night before. My boss wears Bermuda shorts and a short-sleeved shirt. His legs are puffy pink with fuzzy blond hair. All the flesh in the office, except mine, is white, or white blotched with heat rash. They comment on my tan, tease me, tell me I might look "nigger" if I don't watch out.

But I'm forgetting the last employee, so to speak. A black woman slumps on the floor behind our row of teller cages. She is pregnant and very thin. Her bony legs and dusty feet stick out straight from a sack dress, greasy and wearing thin over the lump of baby. From a standing position, I can see only the top of her head, sunk into her chest. On my first morning, I ask for an introduction, but for answer I get smiles and shrugs. At lunchtime one of the women takes orders— hamburger, hamburger with onion, cheeseburger, coke, coke, etc. She shouts to the black woman, who is standing with her head still bowed: "Okay. *Three* hamburgers, *one* with onion, *one* cheeseburger, and *four* cokes. *Got that?* Want me to say it again?" She hands the woman a five-dollar bill and out the back door she scuttles. So I say, "Oh, you pay her to go get your lunch?" More smiles. When she returns, she receives the pennies from the change and slumps down against the wall again.

I am learning not to ask questions, to stifle reaction, to avert my eyes. I postpone until dinner with my husband when I pour it out over the trays of sizzled food. I say, "Do you *know* what we did today all morning—or they did—just because there was no work? They sang hymns, lots of them, all the verses. In their bathing suits. They were jiggling up and down and singing 'Oh, Jesus Wants Me For a Sun . . . beam,' the *beam* up high like this, and 'Come, Come, Come to the Church in the Wildwood' and 'Onward Christian So-ol-diers, Marching As To War,' and what could I do? I tried to sing a bit but it was just too damn weird to be in a bank, so hot, with *her* sitting against the wall, and the boss singing too, in this rotten, foul, hot, surely this is not The United States place. Don't you think?"

"Well," he says, "we won't be here much longer. By

the middle of October, I should be reassigned to Day-ton, Ohio."

Why Dayton, I could ask, but don't. It will all be-come clear or it won't. Though I am here now and will be going there then, I think, I am not, in this new life of mine, supposed to seek reasons for long car trips.

The army assignment is Monsanto Chemical Company, where I check in as assistant to the safety engineer and my husband disappears into rooms where I am not allowed. It is a beautiful, blustery fall, and we rent an un-insulated cabin beside Elm Lake, ten miles outside of Dayton.

In our dwelling, we learn about banking the wood-stove at night, living with mice in our sweaters and cookie boxes, wearing long johns to bed, taking baths half-clothed. We discover chilblains and frostbite. We learn how to stay inside and be cozy, and become devoted observers of ice forming on tree branches, of icicles lengthening into translucent spears that grow from our porch roof. Our landlady warns us that we have to wait until the temperature has been five below for three weeks before we can safely skate on the lake. We buy skates and feel a curious satisfaction at bundling up, slinging our skates over a shoulder, then walking through the snow to the icy stone bench where we don our sliding shoes over three pairs of socks. There are snapping turtles under the ice, and I wonder if our kre-e-ek above them disturbs them in their winter sleep. Do they sleep? There is a swing with a seat set up on the bank and we can swing high and then whoop and let ourselves land any which way on the ice. We improve each weekend until the spring thaw.

On Monday mornings we bank the fire for our return, start the car for its ten-minute warm-up, put on our Monsanto Chemical Company IDs, then coats, mufflers, mittens. My husband seems to grow smaller and more flat as each olive-drab garment affixes itself. Some mornings he looks like a soldier paper doll.

In the entry room at 8:00 A.M., we remove our shoes and put on white overalls that obscure our semi-civilian bodies. White cloth booties enclose our feet. Each Monday morning a nurse pricks one of our fingers for a blood sample. On Fridays, on the way out, we wait for another blood sample to be taken. White count is thus monitored. My husband then vanishes until five o'clock, and I enter my work area, which houses all clerical workers and the safety engineer. We know we are working in a "hot" building and that the pursuit of a "clean" environment is the first priority of our boss. On the right-hand side of his desk is his Geiger counter, on the left, his in-out basket. He is seldom at his desk. He and his machine spend most of each day walking through the building, counting, recording, ticking. His findings are rendered into numbers and sober prose, which are deposited each day in my in-box. I type the reports in six copies (carbon paper) and return them to his in-box.

He is a silent man. We do not chat and when occasionally I ask for clarification of blood-count whiteness or "hot," he blinks his watery eyes and suggests I ask my husband. Does he know that a postwar conscript is not going to open his top-secret mouth unless I bully and weep? Which I do, of course. But I remember only the feeling of victory, not the information. The facts presented seem to have no place to fit in, but like a good secretary (which I am reluctantly becoming) I file them in my mind under a new category—post–atomic bomb health.

In December, my white count falls and I am excused from work, ordered to stay home and to return for a finger prick in five days. My face blooms pimples and there are two boils on my back. My head aches and I am too tired to take advantage of my free time. I keep the fire going and sleep all day beneath additional blankets on loan from the landlady. She brings me hot soup and tells me Californians are simpletons who shouldn't be allowed to leave their state until they've learned a few easy lessons about winter. I need more fat, a reserve to draw on. My husband is even less prepared, so thin and subject to colds, respiratory ailments. I look up at her from my bed—such rosy cheeks, abundant graying hair, clear green eyes, strong stocky legs clad in black wool trousers. This morning I heard her chopping wood, then stacking it on her porch. There is a husband, a truck driver often on the road, and one day I watched their reunion after a brief absence. She is taller than I am and weighs fifty pounds more, yet she ran to him and he picked her up in his arms and carried her to the porch where he slowly set her down and kissed her close and good. Then they disappeared inside their house and the lights did not go on at sunset. As she bends over me, I feel tears coming and close my eyes. I vow to apprentice myself to her if she will allow it, lest we, her California simpletons, die before spring. I don't tell her about our "hot" building. I assume she wouldn't understand, and those who do are not yet allowed to speak about it in public. More potatoes, butter, fresh brown bread, vegetables, she says. You are truly what you eat; she's read that somewhere, and it is certainly true, or true enough.

At the end of my reading, dozing, eating week, my white count is up, my skin looks better, I've gained a few pounds and my headache has receded to a dull ache above my right eye. On Monday, my first day back at work, a female calibrator, who works inside the area off-limits for the office staff, spends the entire day in the office, unable to leave the vicinity of the john. She is having her period in such copious quantities that there is hushed discussion of insisting that my boss drive her to a hospital. She resists. He sets up a cot beside the restroom and goes out to purchase two large boxes of extra-thick Kotex. While he is gone, the telephone operator and I push close to her and learn, in whispers, that she's been bleeding for ten days and, dammit, wishes her body would adjust to her new circumstances or she'll lose her job. She says she always bleeds heavily, but not this much, she must be rundown or something. When she turns over to get more comfortable, I can see blood staining her white booties. This is a new experience, to be in an office with a bleeding woman, my boss sent out to bring in stanching supplies, to know that we will be discussing normal and abnormal menstruation with him as soon as he returns.

I know I am angry and that it has something to do with "hot," lassitude, boils, pimples and headaches. We go back to our desks and await his return. He is a nice man, mild and courteous, but he is a wall around information we suddenly need. We are going to press against him, refuse to do our jobs until we get answers. What is the meaning of "hot," why does it lower your white count, what is the source of the "radiation," and why, if the war is over, are we still working with such materials? He stands beside his desk, his arms around a brown bag of Kotex. He is calm, unswervingly polite as we push closer, our hands darting forward for emphasis. "Hot" means radioactive, exposure produces lowered white count, the source he is not at liberty to reveal, and he hasn't the faintest idea what Monsanto is researching or producing and wouldn't be allowed to tell us even if he knew. At that moment, our patient groans and lurches towards the john. The telephone operator grabs the Kotex bag and holds the door open for her. I glance over at her switchboard and can see five red lights blinking, wires erupting from plug-ins, a headphone set lying over on its side.

Whatthehell. Why am I here? Can I leave? Can my husband?

SPRING 1946
CHAGRIN FALLS, OHIO
LOS ALAMOS, NEW MEXICO

We repack all our belongings in the Oldsmobile in early June, discharged after only
nine months. We drive first to Chagrin Falls, Ohio, to
visit our new friends, physicist Nat Ellis and his wife,
Bette. There, under weeping willows, lying on grass so
green it hurts my eyes, we talk hesitantly, for the first
time, of atomic weapon development, its dangers, the
association of atomic scientists that is forming to raise
questions, force answers. Much of the men's talk is
difficult to comprehend, but Bette and I ask for sim-
plification and they rush to explain, finishing each
other's sentences and laughing frequently at how ea-

ger they are to flush secrets from their minds. They are in civilian clothes, pale from winter light, but handsome again. We lie on our stomachs in the grass, and when the talk dies down, Bette turns towards Nat, climbs on top of him, hugs, kisses, smears him with red, red lipstick. I sit on my husband and tickle him, and then we play leapfrog over to the fishpond. We take off our shoes and socks and wade in the slimy water. We splash each other.

At breakfast, each man states, carefully, that he will not work ever again in weapon research. And then there is nothing more to say and I am left with a feeling of sadness that stings my eyes. Bette hugs me and promises to write. The men shake hands and quietly say good-bye. We wave our hands out the car windows. I cry for the next thirty miles. He asks why. I say I haven't the faintest idea. I say maybe it's because I feel so young and stupid and he is the same age and knows so much more and all that he knows is a pain to him. He squeezes my hand. He says forgetting much of what he's learned is part of his plan for our future.

His honorable discharge and our medical check-outs restore to us a sense of bodily well-being. We aren't sick. We make love again, slowly, giving it time and concentration. We enumerate blessings, naming especially his good fortune in not having been out there to be killed in a perhaps just war. We hope the returning soldiers and sailors can slip back into civilian life and forget their experiences. In an adobe eatery near our motel, we clink wine glasses and toast the future: good health, peace, prosperity. We allow ourselves to get a little drunk.

Still, on the long journey back to our friends and families on the California coast, I feel anxious. To myself, I call my condition "cosmic angst"—a wholly grand term that I learned from Nat Ellis, who said, "I am going to use my cosmic angst against those who do not feel it." "Cosmic" is my favorite word for as large as you can imagine, and "angst"—defined loosely by Nat as "worry"—seems to contain the feeling of nervousness in the choking throat needed to pronounce it, as though I were suffocating in trying to express myself. I often look over at my husband, interrupt my reading to stare at him while he drives, and wonder where he figures in this new feeling. His mother thinks him "fragile," not in a psychic sense—which would have been beyond her—but in his health, his prospects for remaining alive long enough to enter middle and old age. He has absorbed her worries as his own. I often say "Nonsense!" when he complains of a chill coming on, "It's . . ." But I'm not about to give him my new certainty that all over the world something has snapped and that even small children can feel the difference. I don't know any small children but I worry about them anyway.

We head home by way of Los Alamos to spend a weekend with our friends Pete and Kathy. Pete and I have known each other since childhood, our parents being friends. He is a junior physicist and produced plutonium in a Berkeley lab, like my husband, then was drafted and assigned to Los Alamos after the Bomb. When I was about eleven, we lived across the street from each other and one evening after playing kick-the-can, he kissed me. It was like kissing a baseball. His mother held dancing school in their house, and it was there I learned the tango, the waltz, and Doin' the Lambeth Walk. Pete is another only child, sole son. He and Kathy have been married a year, and I can't imagine what she sees in him, she so pert and pretty, he so mother-cocooned.

Kathy is the daughter of a Southern Methodist minister, and I've heard from her own mouth tales about how she got her revenge. She surrendered her virginity at eleven (willingly) to her cousin, made out with every available male thereafter, wore purple lipstick, no underpants, low-cut angora sweaters (she cut them down herself) and pointy bras. She smoked and drank anything offered her. I forget how she made her way to UC Berkeley where she met Pete, but he seems an odd choice. He obviously adores her, that petite figure, the dainty gestures and the crude mouth. She is the first woman I've known who seems to feel that every sentence should shock, if possible. Pete always sits upright nearby, a silly smile on his face. I believe she is his first woman and so different from his mother he probably believes he's discovered a new species. He told us once that when Kathy addresses her mother-in-law, she always speaks like the English lit student she was.

So here's the way it goes in Los Alamos. We are in

their bungalow kitchen and Kathy is fixing dinner. And drinks. She is wearing a maternity smock, pink shorts, and her feet are bare. She lifts her glass to the three of us sitting at the kitchen table and says,

"So, now that our precious bomb-makers have made the fuckin' world safe for bombs, let's drink to their getting off their asses and reversing direction!"

We praise her tomato aspic salad, served first, and she says,

"Pick an ass, any ass. Oppie-ass. They wipe his be-hind and worship the stink."

A cheese-noodle-mushroom casserole: "There's enough plutonium in this glop to satisfy even their appetite for shit-eating."

After her third glass of wine, she says, "The fuckin' baby will arrive glowing blue." Pete delicately backs up his chair. He says, "No, Kathy . . ." and invites my husband to join him in chopping wood while the women make iced coffee that we'll drink on the screened porch. Kathy sips her fourth glass of wine and flings one last sentence at their backs: "It's eighty-four de-grees, but chopping is clean, loud, and the tree's al-ready dead."

WOMEN OFTEN WAIT for their men to leave and then unload, but we clean up in silence. She is not glum and puffs contentedly on a cigarette hanging out one side of her mouth while her hands scrub the casserole dish with a coppery ball. I dry. I'm thinking she hasn't been fair but can't decide just how to say this. I am afraid of her tongue and even more wary of what seems to be an advanced position on issues I've kept fuzzy. I don't understand the blue glow part, but her condition argues against asking her to explain.

After coffee on the porch swings, she curls up beside Pete and goes to sleep, her head in his lap. He strokes her silky brown hair and looks sappy. We drive out of town the next morning.

1949

BERKELEY, CALIFORNIA

REPORT SAYS RADIATION RISK NOT TOLD.
(AP) Workers at nuclear weapons plants before
1950 exposed to cancer risk. . . . Records show that
in the late 1940s and early 1950s, plants making
bomb fuel at Hanford were releasing billions of
dangerously radioactive particles and exposing un-
suspecting people living and working at the site to
the risk of cancer.

Santa Cruz Sentinel, DECEMBER 19, 1989

Molly brought me a black notebook last night
during visitors' hours. She said, "Perhaps you'd
like to write your thoughts since you can't talk." The

cover is blank, no 1949 in gold lettering like her diary, no D I A R Y etched on the cover. It's small enough to slip into my purse and carry with me everywhere. How did she know that I might want to arrange the last three years in words on paper? I want the words to reproach me. She gave no hint of motive. She clucked and soothed and tucked me in. Her sympathy made tears come and then she said she was sorry and poured a glass of orange juice from a bottle she'd brought with her.

I watched Molly closely last night while she was sitting by my bed and the parade of visitors began— my husband, worried, loving, sad; my professor lover, so courteous, his deep voice uttering good wishes for my speedy recovery; Dr. G. checking my chart and saying I could go home in a few days. The dentist would arrive tomorrow morning, he said, to wire my jaw. I shouldn't talk until then. And then there was my graduate student lover, nervous, effusive, carrying a bouquet of pinks and blue iris. Harry, my father, came into the room, jingling the coins in his pocket, looking ready to explode. He got off a few puns and went out into the hall to smoke. My sister said we must talk soon.

Molly is my mother, but I think of her as my confidante and since she knows my deeds, I watched her, hoping I'd find on her face a point of view I could take for my own. But no, she sat there holding her ugly brown leather purse in her lap, her feet placed just so on the floor, and she listened. Occasionally she smiled a tight smile at something her husband said. She sat until everyone had gone and then kissed me on the forehead and murmured, "Tonight you must sleep to get back your strength. And tomorrow, when you have time, write . . . or read."

Writing with the little pen that attaches by clip to my notebook is making me sweat and my hand dampens the page. Perhaps it's fever, though it could also be the listing of visitors. I feel I should explain to the page how one woman could have such an array of well-wishers. Believe me, she's nothing special, not a beauty, and if I say it all happened gradually and in accord with the discovery that men like bold nuttiness, does that excuse me? Does an urge to breed set me apart from mores and manners? No, the words "victim" and "prey" come to mind. I don't like those words. I don't like the person in this bed having her first miscarriage, about to have her broken jaw wired together.

Day before yesterday I was almost three months pregnant, and I started bleeding. I telephoned Molly, and while I was telling her I was bleeding I fainted and crashed onto the terra-cotta tile of the house my husband and I built together. I split my chin (eight stitches) and broke my jaw. I woke up (after a sedative) here in Berkeley's Herrick Memorial Hospital and I'm still bleeding. But it must run its course. If it doesn't, I have to have something called a D and C. When I get out of here or perhaps before I leave, I'll tell my good husband we must get a divorce, enough is enough. We shall never have a child.

WRITING "A CHILD" makes me feel frantic. We began trying three years ago. We were happy enough. He, good to his word, was with a design-engineering firm and loving it. I was in school again, able for the first time to attend full-time without working. We built a house in the hills behind the sixty-inch cyclotron. We built a bedroom for the baby. Now I begin to sound soppy, but it wasn't that way at all. I wanted a baby neutrally, as the next event in life's program, one I hadn't designed but did not oppose. My mother-in-law waited. Everyone began waiting, out there, calling to inquire, then not calling.

A year went by and I found myself more interested in my studies, even developing a passion for, of all subjects, political theory, how governments are formed and why, what the nature of the social contract is. In all this theory there was not a word about babies, and women were never mentioned.

The next year, since we were a serious couple, we followed Dr. G.'s advice and studied ovulation times, took my temperature in the morning, went at it conscientiously when it was up a degree. I asked Dr. G. for a physical exam and he sent air through my tubes and told me I had a tipped uterus. He advised standing on my head after intercourse. He asked if my husband would submit to an analysis of his sperm. Of course, why not?

My husband said to me at the dinner table: "Dr. G. says my sperm have low motility. He says they probably can't make the journey. I should rest more, take vitamins. This may change." I asked about mumps when he was a child because that seemed simpler, kinder, than mentioning Oak Ridge, cyclotrons, plutonium, "hot" environments, but I knew, almost as though I were inside his brain throwing switches to left or right, the thoughts he was derailing.

I told Molly in her garden while she was plucking dead leaves off a fuchsia. It felt good to be there in the sunshine, just the two of us, my father at work, my younger brother at school. We agreed this was not news to spread around, poor man, perhaps he shouldn't even have been told. I said, "Yes, it was no doubt better when a woman could be called barren." She said, "Oh dear, that sounds bitter," and I said no, I didn't feel bitter, just odd, a bit goofy, as though I weren't at all sure what I'd do next. Maybe I'd decide to walk from Berkeley to New York by way of Canada with a dog by my side, something like that.

WHAT WE DID NEXT was artificial insemination.
You take your temperature to find the right time. You
go to the doctor's office. The husband squirts his semen into a bottle in a room by himself. Dr. G. squirts
the semen up high into my passage. We leave quickly
and wait. We do this four times, in four months. Then
we discuss an artificial donor and adoption. We don't
make plans. We stop talking about it.

Dr. G. just stopped by to tell me the jaw wirer has
a conflict of schedule and won't be in until late this
afternoon. He squeezed my hand, said I had passed
fetal tissue and wouldn't need a D and C but was running a slight temp. The hand squeeze was sympathy
and tears came, but I don't mourn the baby that isn't.
I don't deserve sympathy. I'm a monster and I feel I'm
getting out on parole. I didn't tell him this. I wasn't
supposed to talk, and anyway it would have depressed
him. He's Berkeley's childbirth-without-fear doctor.
Mothers form bonds with him, and from me he's had
nothing but trouble. I also have a bond with him, but
both of us want to cut rope and escape.

I write about ten pages, much of it smudged,
whole paragraphs crossed out, as though there's some-

one reading over my shoulder. I can't postpone writing of the "scheme." That's Molly's word. We were sitting at the kitchen table with the bay windows giving a view of canyon eucalyptus and I said, "I'm sort of in love with my professor and one day I asked him if he'd like to help me make a baby because my husband couldn't." Molly sucked in her breath and said, "I'm not sure about that scheme." The word made me laugh, and then she laughed, and for a moment I thought, this mother, this woman at this table, my mother, I don't know enough about her. Anything is possible. And she leaned forward and asked: "What did he say then?" "Well," I said, "he said 'Let me cancel my appointments and we'll go to my place to see if we want to make love.'" Then Molly and I laughed again, and I wondered if there had ever been a daughter and a mother who had exchanged such words.

He took me to his Berkeley apartment in the hills where I had often attended seminars, not quite a graduate student, but almost, too unsure of my knowledge to utter a word. He invited me to lie down beside him, both of us fully clothed, to discover if we wanted to make love, but since I was there, inside the scheme, that's what we did. We took off our clothes and lay naked on his bed all afternoon, his appointments having been canceled. His penis (the second of my life) was tiny, about a third the size of my husband's and not too firm. This didn't seem to make much difference, though I wanted to ask him just what effect this had on his life, his life loving many women and being loved by them. He made that clear in his conversation.

We talked a lot, sometimes naked on our stomachs, and I discovered that I could raise my head and out the window see my parental home across the canyon. Once I saw my tiny mother watering her lilac bushes. We kept to the temperature schedule and met at his apartment only on the two days following ripe time. On my visits with Molly, she would say, "How's the scheme going?" as though it were some kind of new diet, and I'd say, "Fine, but no results yet."

There were times over the next few months when I wanted to call a halt, get free of the effort, the waiting, the deception, taking temperature, times when I found myself wishing I were nine years old, before all this crashed into me. And I wanted a giant moral force to shake my teeth loose. I had a nightmare about Oak Ridge. Three men in white coveralls opened my brain and said, "We have severed your moral fibers. You are now post-atomic," and I said thank you and tried to kiss their hands.

Then I added a third penis, full-size and always hard—on hilltops, in cars with parts of us tangled in the steering wheel. This one was attached to a married graduate student who was father to a little girl whose paternity was in doubt. He vowed, is still proclaiming, that we will find a way, that our love is unique and we'll soon be together forever.

But I don't know. I'm here in this bed and I'm bleeding. I feel the push of blood, hot on the Kotex. Lumpy. I'm getting clean. The moral force has shaken my teeth loose, has broken my jaw, and I can begin to think about a man's body suffering damage because he did his duty, our dead marriage, this ovarian space I inhabit.

Oh, I am so tired. The visitors last night—what did they know? My husband knows about the graduate student and will not recover. He does not know about the professor. The professor doesn't know about the graduate student. Dr. G. knows only what a good doctor ought to know. My father knows nothing. My mother knows all the events and probably more she's not telling. I have no idea who is half author of the fetal tissue oozing from me. Except for a few trifles about the origins of the social contract, I am ignorant. I am beginning to think about my eggs—where they rest, their size, number, shape, their health.

I'm an outcast, though I'm not sure whether this is voluntary or is imposed. I don't deserve company and it is good to be alone. The husband is gone, divorce will be granted. Tears and regret and a final night, a sorrowing, oh-all-is-lost coupling. Cereal, juice and coffee in the morning, last instruction on what I'm to do to improve the real estate while he is gone, wan waves of hands, the green Oldsmobile slowly driving away, then lost from view. His worried parents are paying for his two-month trip to Europe because they believe he will fall apart unless provided with distraction. I know he won't, nor will I. There's something stone-like about both of us now. We get scratched and mottled by acid air, but we don't shatter.

This morning, my first alone in almost five years, I wake to the sun's rays slanting across the double bed. I wriggle to the exact middle, throw off the covers and stretch my arms and legs outward to unfleshed space. I begin reciting a mantra of childhood: I am Candida, twenty-five years old, in this bed, this room, this house, on a hill, high above Berkeley, above the cyclotron, in California, in the country of . . . and then I roll out of bed on his side and wander into the bathroom that looks almost empty without shaving gear, hair grease and the towel with "His" embroidered on its edge (gift of my mother-in-law). I look into the mirror at my sepia face, my long, sun-bleached hair in a tangle. I lift the scissors from the shelf and begin to cut. I cut to a length of one inch all over my head. As I snip and trim, my body grows lighter, gravity weighs less, and yet I feel infinitely extended, easily reaching each room in the house. I fancy I can stand in front of the bathroom mirror and at the same time sit on my piano bench, choose Czerny or Hanon, push down damper or soft pedal. My head takes on the shape of a primitive African statue, my neck joins my collarbone and jaw as though sculpted lovingly by ancestor hands.

In the shower I pour shampoo on my head and rub with fingertips until my scalp aches. "Rub-dub-dub," I say out loud. "House!" I yell. "I'm leaving you!" "You— you" echoes back to me. For a month I've been speaking very quietly, if at all, saving my jaw, and not all that pleased with any of my words. During the three weeks my jaw was wired together and I had to drink salad made liquid in a Mix-Master, I often thought it might be rather pleasant never again to speak, to try to explain, to be sociable. Words from him, from Molly or my father, were an invading army, a tyranny, however kind. Words seemed attached to a previous self. This present self was mute, resting.

I put on a soft, limp Hickory shirt and faded blue jeans with worn knees, my get-to-work costume. I walk barefoot down the long hallway to the kitchen, where the cat rubs my ankles and puts her claws through the frayed material into my knee. I grab her to my chest and step outside through the sliding glass doors to the se-cluded side of the house. There are building materials piled neatly against the huge oak, cans of varnish and linseed oil, cinder blocks stacked logically against the hillside awaiting their destiny as retaining walls, all of which reminds me of the work I've promised to do in the coming months. My assigned tasks are inside work. Rub something called Firzite into all the wood surfaces inside the house that I can reach, soak the tile floors throughout six times with special goop prepared by our Frank Lloyd Wright–obsessed architect (a terra-cotta-tinted preparation that stains my socks red), make burlap curtains for the square living room, make shoji panels of rice paper and redwood frames for the long hallway (Firzite the frames), make window-seat cushions out of orange velveteen, find someone to cart away my Baldwin upright on semipermanent loan, pack up, be gone by the time my ex returns.

All of these tasks are mindless, not difficult—with the possible exception of shoji-making. As I stand clutching the cat against my chest and stare at the two houses being constructed by young couples who are co-pioneers carving house sites into cliffs at low cost, on the land above the sixty-inch cyclotron, land that has always been considered impossible to hang a house on, I feel I'm losing the only community I've ever belonged to.

Our friendships have been forged gradually through common problems with city regulations, the insane bulldozer operators, the occasional danger of fire starting below on the dry hills and sparking swiftly up, the hoses manned by all residents, the fire engines trying to make time up narrow Panoramic Way. Poison oak eradication. Different though we are from each other in talent, education, style, we are all post-war (1948/49) graduates seeking a newness, a forgetting, a settling into odd jobs or professions or study, naming hawk species, trying to beget children, swooning at sunsets with the Golden Gate and Bay bridges in our grateful view. We know how lucky we are, we know we should be content.

Our discontent surfaces every weekday at 5:00 P.M. at Marty and Glo's tiny bohemian apartment I can now see across the oak- and madrone-studded canyon. Marty is our carpenter/contractor, barely five foot three, and Glo is his wife. They met while working at the shipyard in Richmond during the war and their romance began, so they say, when Marty was whistling a Bach partita and Glo chimed in with contralto counterpoint. He's from poor folk in New Haven, Connecticut, Polish, and she's a reserved graduate in math from UC Berkeley. She wears her thin brown hair in a bun, never a speck of makeup. She tut-tuts when Marty utters socialist dogma (we all agree more or less with him but wouldn't state our opinions so baldly), and when we fall into gossip and wonder what's going on with this female or another and Marty again says "What she needs is a guy to take her into the bushes. . . ." Glo laughs with the rest of us, says, "Oh Marty, really."

I can't remember why it became the custom for us to gather after work or school at their apartment, but we've been sitting on their floor cushions at five or five-thirty for over a year. Diana (English) and David are usually there, and Janet, who is trying to conceive. She has a glottal stop in her speech and we tease her. She says it's because she's Jewish; we say it's because she's from Brooklyn. Marty says, "There's a differ-ence?" Several times a week Judd arrives. He's been liv-ing on upper Panoramic Way for years, and since he's related to Isadora Duncan and can tell us stories about the Berkeley Temple of the Winds, he regards all of us as carpetbaggers.

Glo serves fragrant homemade cinnamon rolls,

coffee and red wine. Sometimes we can persuade Glo and Marty to play their instruments for us, Glo the cello, Marty the violin, or Marty, who paints wild cubist oils, will rant about modern art, how it's the only art since the Renaissance that "talks." We argue, shout at each other, make what Marty calls "hoo-haw fun." My community.

One day my husband and I walk over to their apartment, slump down silent on the cushions, listen, laugh a bit, nibble a few bites, put the remainders of our buns back onto the paper plates. Marty says to my husband, "We're going to break ground on our house next week, crack a bottle of champagne, you goin' to be around?" My husband squirms, sits up straight and says, "No, we're here to tell all of you that we're getting a divorce. I'm leaving in a few days for Europe and she'll stay to do work on the house, then move out."

The silence that falls on all of us is so total I can hear the water drip down through the filters in the coffee pot. I stare at my feet and my toes poking out of shredded tennis shoes, once white now gray and mottled with paint and glue and old mud. And then they are all talking at once, not consoling, angry.

"WHY? How stupid can you get?! So you had a miscarriage, so try again!" (Marty)

"This is unforgivable. I do not understand." (Glo)

"I'm going to cry. Or scream." (Janet)

"You are both insane. You think it's better out there? What dunces!" (Judd)

"I don't understand either. Are you asking us to UNDERSTAND?" (Diana)

"I am completely out of words. They are gone!" (David)

"So I work my ass off building you a house, and you guys help, and we're FRIENDS, and WHO THE HELL's goin' ta live in the goddamn fuckin' house?" (Marty)

"Marty, please." (Glo)

"But I'm so mad I could vomit. Jee . . . sus?! What a goddamn waste." (Marty)

WE STAND AND SAY GOOD-BYE. They don't telephone and I almost know why but not quite.

A few days after my ex-husband leaves, I see the green Oldsmobile parked down below the house on the dusty road, a white piece of paper tucked under the windshield. My in-laws, without alerting me, have driven two cars, parked one, departed in the other. The note says, "Keys under the seat. Hope you are well." This car is mine through the divorce settlement; the house with its loan payments is his, which is as it should be since I don't plan to earn more than maintenance now or in the future. The tank is full (my in-laws are always technically virtuous) and since I'm low on milk, bread and fresh vegetables, I fetch my purse and drive to the market, then to my parents'

garden, which I've promised to water while they are at
the cabin in the Sierras. After watering, I take their mail
into the house and wander through the silent downstairs, taking in Molly's placement of orange next to
red next to maroon, suddenly a patch of blue in a vase
with sun rays casting the blue onto an oriental rug.
Then into my father's den, where he writes a daily col-
umn for the *San Francisco Call Bulletin*. There are books
shelved to the ceiling, a huge dictionary open on a
stand, and his maximum-size Underwood on his desk.
Stale tobacco smell in this room but not in the rest of
the house because Molly won't allow it. At the end of
a row of books just above his desk is *Pilgrim's Progress,*
the spine worn, a faded red. I know this work is a clas-
sic and since a life goal of mine is to read all the classics, even the Christian ones, I pull it off the shelf,
pour myself a glass of stale orange juice, and curl up
on the sofa in the living room.

Copyright 1903. Born 1628, died 1688. Spent twelve
years in prison for his beliefs but did not write his
book there, as legend tells, but later when he was free
to wander and preach, annoying everyone. He names
his pilgrim Christian, which trips me for a bit, but on

page 23, while Christian is walking with Pliable, a companion who has agreed to go with him because Christian has promised him happiness if he will but follow his lead, they both fall into "a very miry slough" called Despond. They are "grievously bedaubed with dirt . . . and began to sink into the mire."

I feel a shiver of laughter rising through my body, flung at my body from the brittle pages, daring me to step down into the Slough of Despond with Christian, struggle to get out. With my finger marking the page, the book pressed against my thigh, I head for my father's dictionary to look up the pronunciation of "slough." Is it sluf, slow, slew, slof, which? As my feet in socks slip and slide over the polished hardwood floors, around the corner into the den, I'm rooting for the hint of disgust in the long *o*'s of slew and there it is, not the first choice, which is "slou" as in "out," but the second, rendered "sloo" and I say it out loud, letting the oo take a long time until it meets the martial "despond" and we're all stuck, sinking in the mire.

Back on the sofa, I read on until the sun leaves the blue vase, and the deep comfort of the room, where every object has been chosen carefully, all wood polished without blemish, every aspect planned, begins to fret me and make me hungry for the outside. I tuck the book under my arm and lock up, reminding myself to tell my father that I will return it when I've finished reading it.

As I drive up Marin Avenue towards Tilden Park, I'm pleased to be inside the green Oldsmobile climbing the Hill of Difficulty, leaving behind the City of Destruction. At Tilden, I pause at a trail and lace my tennies more tightly because the trail descends surely into the Valley of Humiliation. I still clutch my book and though I see no one ascending, I hope to meet Worldly Wiseman or Pliable or Hypocrisy, who was born in the land of Vainglory. Any of these talkative gentlemen would serve to test my new name against their considerable wit. After fifty pages with Bunyan, while back on the sofa, I knew my name was Barren Woman.

I'm feeling surprisingly cheerful and very pleased with my new game. Again, as with my release from unnecessary head hair, I feel light, so light that I hold onto a red madrone branch lest I float from the ground. I'm a trifle sad that my name is a condition rather than a quality, but my plan is for Candida to have conversations with Barren Woman, and I'm sure certain qualities related to that condition will emerge. I'm afraid that Barren Woman is determined to search for the cause or causes for her condition and to continue the search until she gets satisfactory answers. This will be up the Hill of Difficulty endlessly. Candida may not agree that this is wise or healthy or reasonable and may question Barren Woman's sanity. I know now that they are henceforth separate from each other and can discuss, argue, find flat areas of clover and grass where they can walk barefoot.

AS THE SUMMER WANES and I finish most of the tasks given me (as penance), I am eager to leave this melancholy house and establish residence near the campus, close to my job as hostess in a popular restaurant called The Black Sheep. I find a room with cooking privileges in a house filled with graduate students. The landlady lives elsewhere. The room faces a back garden; the bed is narrow, the ceiling high, the desk wide and sturdy. I can move in the day after Labor

Day. I have only the shojis to complete. They are giving me a lot of trouble—the rice paper tears, the frames streak with glue, the constructions wobble and won't slide smoothly on the tracks.

I'm still reading Bunyan, rationing myself to a few pages a day because I don't want to get to the last page. Again and again he makes me laugh, and I know he intends me to find his adventures both instructive and amusing. Something about my ongoing journey at Christian's side alerts me to portents, a belief and a habit I thought I'd left back in childhood. Example: If the mockingbird wakens me at six, today the glue, rice paper and frames will embrace the *idea* of shoji and, almost without my hands interfering, will come to-gether in harmony. If this doesn't happen, then the mockingbird was just a bird singing.

One morning after packing a few boxes to take to my rented room, placing them next to the sliding doors for ease of exit, I pour myself another cup of coffee and step outside to greet the sun, now separat-ing from wispy fog.

"Candida! Candeeda! Are you home?"

Oh no, no people. No one is welcome here, no

friends, no family. This is my private place; no one may enter here. But a tall, thin young man gallops up the dirt path and skids to a stop when he sees me. "Hi!" he says. He begins yanking green leaves off a bush. He looks foolish standing there in dirty pants, dusty sandals, a torn gray T-shirt, uninvited. I try to remember where I've seen him before. His face is hidden by masses of dirty, yellow curls as he concentrates on stripping the greenery.

"Judd's my uncle. I'm working on his house. Over there." He points across the canyon. "My name is Durevol."

I remember something my parents told me . . . an article and picture in the local paper about a Durevol, son of the town's most eccentric couple. He had no formal schooling but had won a county architectural competition. $1,500 prize.

"Oh yeah. You won a contest."

"Judd said your husband might have some building work for me to do."

"I don't have a husband. He's gone, and I'll be gone too, in a few weeks." He looks about to collapse standing there, plucking leaves. "Do you want some orange juice?"

"Thank you." He sits down on a cinder block near his bush and stares out over the trees. While filling a pitcher with orange juice and placing two glasses and the pitcher on a tray, I spy on him. Impossible that he could win something. He looks about sixteen, forlorn, dazed. I carry the tray over to him and he stands as I approach. He doesn't reach for his glass of juice. I have to put the tray on the ground and extend it to him. He doesn't seem to notice the glass is in my hand but suddenly he smiles. He's pulling leaves again and staring at me.

"You cut your hair."

"Do you want your juice or not?" He conveys his lack of interest in juice by a graceful half turning-away of his body, one arm following the turn, like a dancer on a stage.

"I'm a sculptor. May I . . . would you let me . . . could I sculpt your head?" I want to say no, sharply, but something about his green eyes tells me that he's offering me his talent as innocently as the sun offers warmth. I wonder how he knows my hair is different. Where have his eyes been when I've thought myself unobserved? Did he watch me from Judd's house? How many other eyes can reach me from balconies on the hillside? I shiver and button my cardigan up to my chin while I say, "I don't like people to look at me. I could never sit for you while you sculpt my head. I would hate it."

"You wouldn't have to sit," he answers quickly, not pleading. "You could just go on with what you do, walk around, anything, and I would work."

"But why . . . ?" I almost ask, "Why *my* head?" but realize my vanity. I might as well ask him why he walks or talks. I know he will not fuel others by giving compliments, or by ranking heads in a hierarchy of artistic allure. "I wouldn't have to wear anything special, or look different, or stop what I'm doing?"

"I told you. May I? I could start today. I work about an hour and then stop. I work when that's what I want to do. Maybe an hour today, an hour tomorrow, every day until I can work without you. Then only when I get stuck . . . would I need you."

Fresh green leaves, more and more of them, are

falling to the ground. This effort at controlling my future is tiring me. "Okay. You may start whenever you wish. I'll be home all day."

His hands pull away from the stalk. He buries his fingers in his greasy, yellow curls and presses in on his temples with the palms of his hands, a familiar technique to ease migraines. He doesn't say thank you or good-bye or see you later, but turns and runs down the dusty path without looking back at me.

EVERY DAY HE COMES. The first day he arrives toting a pillowcase filled with plasticene and sets up in a corner of the square living room. He rarely speaks to me, but on the days when he stays only fifteen minutes and sits mutely beside his emerging head, staring out the window, I am aware that there is something about me that does not please him. I have no idea what that might be and although we never refer to our original agreement, I sense on those occasions that he would like me to "sit" for a brief time. When he leaves each day, it is always without a farewell.

One day he abruptly stops his work and although

a Brandenburg Concerto is surging through the stereo speakers, he sits down at the Baldwin and begins vigorously playing something with startling louds and liquid softs and much chasing of fingers up and down the keys. The piano does not accommodate the harpsichord, but neither are they at war with each other. When the tape is over, he continues, subdued and lyrical. So tender and lingering is the finale that the cat's purr can be heard. He lifts his hands and turns towards me.

"I've written an opera—with a ballet—all the instruments and all the dances." This isn't a boast; there is no pride in the telling. Just a fact or two.

"It's not fair," I tease, feeling an unusual peace with him after his concert. "You're a designer of buildings, almost an architect, a painter, a sculptor, and now a musician. I can't do any of those things. I've had lessons, but I can't really even play my own Baldwin. I'll bet your parents never made you take piano lessons. I've heard that your mother *danced* during the big Berkeley fire. Probably no one forced you to *do* anything or *be* anybody, so you just grew and did things, and here you are! You didn't even have to go to school or wear shoes, did you?"

He turns back to the keyboard and strikes two chords, one low, one high, then stands up.

"Not *almost* an architect. *Am* an architect. I'm a dancer and in December I'm going to New York to dance with a company. I will then not have time to do anything else."

I try to picture this improbable young man huddled into a winter coat, blond curls darkened by city grime, fair skin pinched and pasty-white. He sits again, his long, thin arms stretching to hug the length of keyboard, and then his fingers pound high notes in a brief segment so fast his hands blur. He jumps up, leaps and spins around the room, dances to the music still in his memory. Back and forth from piano to space, bending over the piano bench, springing to window seats, dipping, shuddering, falling to one knee, the music softening, fading, the dancer standing in the middle of the room, perspiration dripping from his chin, his head bowed.

As he hurries to leave, he hands me a watercolor-

and-ink painting he has pulled from the pillowcase of plasticine. He does not explain or ask for praise. After he is gone, I place the somewhat crumpled painting on the kitchen table. I admire the intricacy of images, the subtle blending of blacks, grays, pale green, but cannot shake the feeling that it is a chaotic scene, blending butterflies and rockets. Is this how he sees the world?

In the days that follow his concert, he works on my head with more speed than before. It seems to me to be almost finished. I am growing fond of it and begin to want to keep it with me, something I had not imagined when he began to pluck and pull out a nose, carve an ear, do and redo the mouth, fret over the eyes, which wouldn't come alive to his touch. The boxes piled neatly near the sliding doors are a statement to the silent sculptor, were he to notice, that our time is ending, and so must the work on the head. The two of us, working quietly almost side by side, but not together, the sunshine on the dusty tile, belong to this house and cannot be carried down the hill to my tiny room. I hope he knows this.

One evening, after I've been given the key to my

new dwelling, I pack a few boxes and a suitcase into the car and drive down the hill to my room. I Lysol the toilet, tack batiks to the walls, and decide to sleep in my narrow bed this night rather than drive back up the hill to a house I feel I've already left. The contraction of space pleases me, city sounds outside, life around me again. No reminders of small failures. In the morning, I choose a place on the bookcase, in the sunlight, where the head can sit. People—who?—will ask about it. I needn't answer, but will smile an unrevealing smile to match the head's enigmatic expression.

It is nearly noon when I drive back up the hill, park the car on the road below the cantilevered living room, walk slowly up the path Durevol took a month ago and every day since. The cat nervously rubs against my jeans, flicks her tail, runs ahead, comes back, urging me towards a feeding. When I slide open the glass doors, the cat, instead of scooting into the kitchen as is her habit, lets out a throaty growl and hightails it into the bushes.

I step towards the living room and stop. The sculpted shoulders—*my* shoulders—with a twisted stump of neck, are as usual sitting on spread-out newspapers in the corner of the room. Even as I blink to restore the missing head, fear ethers from my shoulders to my arms, through my chest and down. Ten feet from me, the head lies on one ear, deep holes in the tufted hair, nose smashed on one side, eyes staring straight ahead, never so alive as they seem now in death.

I run out the open glass doors, down the path, stumbling over my distant feet. I hug the warm hood of my car, feel oddly sleepy, slip down into the soft dirt beside the car and close my eyes. A cool breeze lifts the hairs on my bare arm; the sun releases the scent of bay and eucalyptus.

*The first giant cyclotron was built by Earnest
Lawrence, the father of all cyclotrons, on a hill near
Berkeley in California, immediately after the
Second World War. It was safer to stay away from
habitation, Lawrence felt, because such a big
cyclotron would send out deadly radiations while
operating. Other universities also planned to build
cyclotrons away from campuses.*
LAURA FERMI, *ATOMS IN THE FAMILY*,
UNIVERSITY OF CHICAGO PRESS, 1954

I n the fall of 1949, in my room off campus, I feel
myself coming alive again, being present for the
sight of leaf colors, rushing from jobs to class (Political Theory, Milton, Masterpieces of English Lit.),
studying until 1:00 A.M., falling onto my narrow bed,
sleeping without dreams, going out the door at 7:00

A.M., into the stream of students who seem in no hurry to arrive anywhere.

Sometimes I feel a twitch of annoyance. Why do I never overhear the words "bomb" or "atom bomb" or "Hiroshima"? The students seem so thoughtlessly young, and I, at twenty-five, feel myself to be already an elder, one who knows but is not consulted.

Early in October, my favorite California month, I am on my way to class, wearing my pink linen dress, my floppy sandals, when the graduate student who said "We'll find a way, our love is unique" matches his stride to mine and asks, "Where have you been?" I've been looking for you. Calling you." He looks so handsome in his white shirt, his beige officer pants so sleek with no pleats, carrying a briefcase, which identifies him as not quite a professor, perhaps a teaching assistant, a notch above student. He drops the briefcase onto the sidewalk and pulls me into a whole body embrace there on Telegraph Avenue. Instantly I am in love, comically, utterly, uniquely.

There are problems, of course, but problems are the seasoning for true love. If no one objects, why do it? My parents think I've gone crazy. His parents in Portland, Oregon, believe he's departed from the moral path of his marriage and fatherhood. His wife and daughter move to his parents' home while they wait for him to come to his senses. We brood and fret and rent a furnished apartment on University Avenue.

Immediately we find ourselves consumed by the Year of the Oath. We pass out leaflets, meet with others in the Shattuck Hotel and plot strategy. Who is the enemy? The state? The regents? The signers? Who is signing? Who is not signing? Can he sign but still be considered loyal to the idea of academic freedom? Must he refuse to sign and lose his teaching assistant position? If his professor leaves the university, can he follow him to wherever he goes?

The oath, included in our leaflets, reads this way:

> I do solemnly swear that I will support the Constitution of the United States and the Constitution of the State of California, and that I will faithfully discharge the duties of my office according to the best of my ability: that I am not a member of the Communist Party, or under any oath, or a party to

any agreement, or under any commitment that is
in conflict with my obligations under this oath.

I muse, but do not utter, "The holy government
says to the physicists—*If you reveal the secrets we know you
have you will be charged with treason;* to the professors—
Swear that you have no secrets, or be fired."

Meanwhile, my father writes a scathing article
published in his San Francisco newspaper and returns
his diploma to the university, an act that makes him
briefly a local hero. George Stewart, an English professor, is chosen by a group of nonsigners to write the
events while they are unfolding. His book, *The Year of
the Oath,* tells the story but identifies no nonsigner by
name, a decision arrived at by consensus. He alone
will absorb the flack. What does he have to lose? He
has a book. On page one, he writes:

In that year we went to oath meetings, and talked
oath, and thought oath. We woke up, and there was
the oath with us in the delusive bright cheeriness
of the morning. "Oath" read the headline in the
newspaper, and it put a bitter taste into the break-

fast coffee. We discussed the oath during lunch at the Faculty Club. And what else was there for subject matter at the dinner table? Then we went to bed, and the oath hovered over us in the darkness, settling down as a nightmare of wakefulness.

Then, in the hours of the night, Academic Freedom and all the other high ideals drew far off and seemed small, and each man or woman, alone, faced "Sign-or-Get-Out!" in terms of next month's bills, or the daughter to be kept in college, or the payments on the house and the baby due in the summer, or the ever-recurrent thought, "At my age, could I get another job?"

In our apartment we continue our academic work, writing what we have to write, loving, quarreling, cooking, occasionally entertaining, hosting fervent, feverish oath arguments. In the spring, his professor, a nonsigner, announces that he is leaving to take an appointment at the Princeton Institute for Advanced Study. He will welcome any student of his who can follow him; all of his students are cravenly devoted to him and can't imagine life out from under his guidance. My man, the man who I'm sure has never inhabited a "hot" environment, applies to Princeton University and is accepted. Will I be going with him? Is that a wise decision? We shall have to pretend to be married at Princeton because his divorce has not yet begun.

We lurch into summer, still undecided, but sure we can't live without each other. My mother calls to tell me that Margaret, a mother of two small, blonde, curly-haired little girls, who built a house on the ridge above the house I have left, has just died of malignant melanoma, age twenty-four.

He flies to Portland to say good-bye to his wife and the child (who may not be from his loins, he says) to beg his parents to understand, and then on to Princeton. I pack the car with our clothes and many books. I drive night and day to the East Coast, fleeing from, towards.

1950-53

PRINCETON, NEW JERSEY

*All plants and animals are made from cells. The
cells of the human body are differentiated according
to function. There are cells which make up bone,
muscle, blood. Cells which create immunity, send
messages from one part of the body to another, cells
which remember, understand, see.*

SUSAN GRIFFIN, *CHORUS OF STONES*, page 68

I don't have much time, only four days of his absence, to consider my situation here in Princeton.
To ask myself, how did I get into this pickle? Here I
am, in this man's town (no female students), support-

ing him, doing my labor for medieval scholarship, cooking gourmet, typing his manuscripts (clean copy, no errors allowed), trying to be "good in bed" (three times a day: upon awakening, before dinner, and just before or during sleep). He has theories, and one of his theories is that orgastic potency is necessary for good health and full womanhood. If I (a woman) were allowed into Firestone Library, I might find a volume that made the same claim for celibacy.

Lovely word, that.

It's late November 1952, and it's snowing outside our two-bedroom box. My husband has gone to Oregon to amuse his lunatic Catholic father, who has suffered another heart attack. Planes could be grounded and I might not have my four days. He might return early and say, "Well, what have you been doing? Seen anyone?" He might phone, say he loves me, ask if his paper is typed yet, ask if I've found another job. Two days ago I lost the best job for a female in Princeton— private secretary to Dr. George Gallup, sixty dollars a week. The phone is in the closet under two pillows, his paper to be typed is just where he left it, on his desk.

Although I have resolved to spend some of my ex-

quisite solitude in figuring out the pickle, I am also
going to write an article about getting fired for wearing a huge Stevenson button just outside Dr. Gallup's
office during the Stevenson vs. Eisenhower campaign
for president. I have proof that Nixon met Gallup in
the Nassau Tavern and learned from the pollster that
Americans are soft in the head about dogs, cloth
coats, military service, and remorse, and that Nixon
used this material in his Checkers speech. I have documents (lifted from filing cabinets) that prove Gallup's
aid to the Republicans (a pollster no-no), and if my
husband will just tend his papa for the full four days,
I'll write a whistle-blowing piece that surely will be
snapped up by *Reporter* magazine.

Then what? Then I'll be able to claim, suddenly,
that I'm a writer and should have space and time for
writing, that I am not a body slave or a gourmet cook,
that medieval scholarship has too many footnotes, that
I'm getting older and should find out if my eggs are
undamaged, that love has an anxious face and is tired.

I exist in an environment of concepts that have
the tenacity of weeds and like weeds have grown up
around me without a gardener's selective ordering of

nature. My brain is a jungle. What grows there? I came here of my own accord, following Romantic Love. A man must work hard to prepare himself for a Career, and his wife will show her love by doing everything in her power to help him achieve his goal—cook, type, work, lie with him, postpone children. Women are Helpmates; men are Thinkers with Needs.

Writing the above paragraph has given me a headache. I get lots of headaches here in Princeton. My putative husband's father is an allergist and my headaches have been discussed by letter. He's advised skin patches, tests, but I know that a headache gives me time in a darkened room, alone. I lie flat on the bed with a wet, cold washcloth over my eyes and have insistent visions of men marching ever forward, the women three steps behind, growing smaller, weaker, grasping shirttails, crying, begging, falling away, being replaced by others. At such moments, what we have together, how we've arranged it, he and I, appears not to be chosen, but given. Society's plan for this decade. Uniformed figures appear along the road. I can't detect their gender. They carry guns or placards with slogans: Support your man! Have orgasms! Be pretty! Type clean copy! His success shall be your reward!

In my more cheerful moments I know that a spell has been cast over me. He is handsome, smart, funny; his skin is olive, his teeth white and if I were to loosen my grasp, women would come running to do his errands and lie beneath him. I would crash into a single state, twenty-nine years old, divorced, without career, inert in anomie-land. Having no male to reflect skin, dress, hair, smooth legs, shaved armpits, I would instantly shrivel into old-maid age. Unwanted. Without children. A discard.

Why is it that I relinquish control over my thoughts when he is near me? Just today, after buying bread, peanut butter, celery and milk for a planned stint at the typewriter, I slipped into the Episcopal chapel on campus to listen to the organist practice the Goldberg Variations. I felt disloyal, almost unfaithful, but sank into the purple velvet pew, shut out surroundings (the town, the university), forgot him, let my worries bleed into vibration and sound.

Through splitting or fission, the ionization of cells
leads to a chain of microscopic events, which one
may witness in the end as death by cancer or the birth
of a deformed child.

SUSAN GRIFFIN, *CHORUS OF STONES*, page 193

I n late spring of 1953, he gets his reward. He passes
his orals, *summa*! We live in barracks built to house
soldiers during World War II and we call our settlement Fertile Valley because there are so many children popping out of the wives of graduate students.
Their older siblings play tag around our house while
their mothers nurse the new babies. I ask one little
girl whether her mother had a boy or a girl last week.
She stares at me for a moment and then says, "I don't
know. . . . It doesn't wear any clothes. My father stays
at the library all the time. He's got the orals. Does
your father have the orals?"

His second reward is a Fulbright grant to Germany beginning in September. I do not want to go to Germany, a country I regard as permanently polluted. His second area of interest, however, after medieval history, is the Nazi scourge. His mother is a Jew; he wants to pick the scab.

In June I miss a period and immediately my stomach declares war. He doesn't seem to notice that I'm artfully shoving food around on my plate and nibbling constantly on soda crackers. I cheer myself by chanting "Hooray! Morning sickness!" in the bathroom.

I postpone telling him because even I, in my potentially happy state, realize that this is not an ideal time to be pregnant. I continue daily to wade through the swamp air of my walk to my job as secretary to Professor Oskar Morgenstern. It is the hottest summer in Princeton's history. The professor is known for his work on the gold standard and game theory and is seldom in the office or even in the state. Where he is or goes is a secret, and I won't know for years that he is busy working with John von Neumann on the hydrogen bomb.

My job is to type his graduate students' papers, and there's a special typewriter with mathematical symbols instead of the customary keyboard. The humidity curls the paper, locks the machine in sludge and causes one student to lie down in front of the fan and mutter, "Fuck. Fuck. S'cuse me. Fuck!"

My only amusement at work is the undergrad who delivers the mail each day. He's stuck at Princeton for the summer because he's poor and is something of a charity student. He's in the English Department and wants to be a writer. He writes thousands of words a day that he delivers to me and then retrieves the following day, after receiving from me a reaction, a stray comment, a kind word. His words are typed single-spaced on yellow paper, four or five pages a day, perfect spelling and grammar, without paragraphs. Daily, I peer into an uncaged mind that travels from philosophy and literary criticism to his love affair with his sister. Far from causing him guilt, all this complexity has convinced him he should bring her to Princeton in the fall, that they should pretend to be married and live in student housing. He's a pretty young man with rampant acne and a Prince Myshkin smile. I like him more than anyone I've met in the three years I've been in New Jersey.

Preparing for our exit from the United States, we travel to Elkton, Maryland, to marry. We can't marry in Princeton because this event would be noted in the local newspaper and that would be a perhaps unpleasant surprise to the Princeton administration. The deed is performed by a drunken marrying-preacher who slouches against the wall of city hall and approaches cars, asking the driver, "Want to get married? Ten dollars, ten minutes." We marry not because of the pregnancy, but because we want our passports to wear the same last name, having heard that in Germany landlords might not approve of American looseness.

Back in our barracks house, I confess pregnancy; we argue about money and how can we possibly support a child? He suggests abortion and then vigorously urges it. I pretend to consider this but know I'll never, never agree. Already I tenderly place my hands over where it grows and talk to it, sing, say over and over again, "I dwell in Possibility. . . ." He backs off and we concentrate on getting rid of everything we own, selling tables, chairs, bookcases, clothes, beds, couches, and finally, the car.

There's a war going on in Korea and a week before

we depart on the USS *Veendam,* he receives greetings from the U.S. Government—welcome to the Intelligence Corps, designation first lieutenant. He tears the stiff white paper into tiny scraps and throws them into the waste basket. If they want him, he mutters, they'll have to find him.

1953–55
MUNICH, GERMANY

German is a language I have not studied except in Mark Twain. On shipboard I try—German grammar open on my lap, myself wrapped in blankets in a deck chair, husband at my side coaching. But halfway through conjugation of the verb *to be* I feel my meager breakfast migrating up to my throat and I rush to the railing to throw up. We bring a bucket to the side of the chair so all I have to do is lean over. Everyone on board is seasick except my husband, who roams the decks trying to find someone to chat with. Eleven days of this and then Rotterdam and trains and finally Munich, where everyone speaks German and I feel much better.

Munich is a city still ravaged by Allied bomb damage, but the Germans are rebuilding with good humor night and day. They are under American jurisdiction, and our passports get us out of difficulties every day. We obey or comply with their rules only if we wish to. We find an apartment in Schwabing, the artist section, and realize only after moving in that they are building it while we are inhabiting it. The workers wander through our rooms saying "Excuse me, *bitte schoen*," and we lower our gaze, shrug our shoulders.

The leaves fall, the snow and ice arrive, I get bigger and bigger. I leave the apartment once each day in my stadium boots, my green winter coat that I've come to hate, my long johns and the pregnancy skirt with the front cut out that Molly sent to me. I go in search of fresh vegetables besides cabbage, fruit of any kind, pork and lamb, more potatoes. I balance my unstable body with two string bags, trying not to fall on the ice. Our gums are bleeding and we believe we have scurvy from a sudden lack of orange juice. I get a cinder in one eye and it turns red and full of pus. The Germans call this the *bose blick,* the evil eye, and cross the street when they see me waddling down the sidewalk.

In January, we locate Dr. Lohmer, Bavaria's child-birth-without-fear gynecologist/obstetrician. He's magnificent—tall, handsome, kind, he's a passionate skier. We're about even on language: He speaks a bit of English; I a bit of German. He understands my English and I almost understand his simple German. He pronounces me fit and swabs my eye, finds the cinder and extracts it, gives me a soothing wash solution to apply every day. He gives lectures throughout Germany about ways to deliver a baby without drugging the mother and is usually booed off the stage. He estimates March 15 as my due date.

We buy a bassinet and soft blankets that fit snugly. It has wheels and I practice rocking it, wheeling it into the kitchen, the bedroom. We buy diapers and baby clothes, receiving blankets. We discuss names, Mical if it's a girl, and of course he wants a son named after him and his father, the third in line. I lie down whenever possible and sleep, sleep, sleep, between kicks. Our apartment is just barely warm enough for existence and we're throwing our entire Fulbright stipend into the tile oven to maintain adequate warmth. I switch to tennis shoes when I go outside, for better traction on the sidewalks. In a store one day, a German woman tells me that wearing flat shoes will damage the baby. I should be wearing heels! I add this to the lore I'm collecting, like the Germans' belief that cat skins draped over one's shoulders will cure the flu. I realize I've not seen a cat anywhere, many dogs but no cats.

We visit Dr. Lohmer again on February 15, for a checkup. He examines me, blood pressure, etc., then moves to a corner of the room to talk to my husband. I can't hear what they are saying in German but am not curious, nor do I find this ominous. Probably they are discussing payment, how much and when.

In the ninth month I am a dreaming body, so huge and unwieldy that my husband takes over the shopping and most of the cooking. He is tender and loving, and I especially like our nights when he lies against my back with one arm draped across my belly, his hand gently caressing the baby's shape, his lips kissing my neck. The baby has moved down and shifts from side to side. I'm sure it is Mical and I see her lying beside me, a pink mouth seeking my breast. A perfect girl.

I am standing in the kitchen when suddenly the

water spills from inside me, puddling on the cold floor, soaking my long johns, my wool socks. My white socks are tinged pink, which I realize is blood from inside where the baby is. The "breaking of the waters" that I've read about in books is now an experience I'm having, the event signaling the opening wide of my body, the pushing, sliding tyranny of birth. The first intake of air, the first cry. I smile at my husband and hug him, suddenly shy of expressing my joy at seeing pink water on the kitchen floor.

Labor is beginning. I find the slow building towards bearable pain fascinating and want to tell him but can't find the words. I don't remember how we get to the clinic, certainly not in a car, not on a bus. We don't know anyone who has a car. The police in Munich ride horses or walk. At the clinic I am alarmed that Dr. Lohmer is skiing on Zugspitze and will return in a few hours. The midwives are there. They quickly lead me to a surgical bed and bid me rest and breathe steadily. Midwives are, in Germany, required as part of the team for births; doctors are not. One midwife massages my stomach and I feel a sting in my buttock. I clutch my husband's hand and ask "What was that?"

and he says, "Nothing. Just lie back." Everyone in the room knows we do not want any drug to dull the pain. They know I want to see, hear, feel all the way to a child pushing her way into life with breath.

I OPEN MY EYES to see Dr. Lohmer and my husband bending over me. They are fuzzy; each holds a hand. My mouth slurs, "Mical? The baby?" I pull one hand away and feel my almost flat stomach. They rush to tell me, saying together, ". . . dead for three weeks . . . malformed skull . . . didn't want you to see . . . a girl . . . decomposed . . . you have a high fever . . . must rest and stay here until you are well . . . take care of you . . . have another whenever . . ." I struggle with "You knew?" Louder, at my husband, "*You* knew?" I see his tears when he bends his head to my cheek. I yell, "I want to see her! Show me Mical! Where is she?"

During the ten days I remain at the clinic and they save my life with penicillin, I dream often of Mical and she is never decomposed, she is living with another couple, she is wading in the ocean, she is sucking my breast. I hear babies crying in other rooms in the clinic and I know it is Mical who is crying. If only I could get up and go to her.

Three months later, when I have a job with the American Committee for Liberation from Bolshevism, Inc. (an American government propaganda radio station), I am again pregnant. I cry, and cry much more, and beg Dr. Lohmer for an abortion. Abortion is illegal in Bavaria, but he finally consents, trusting us. The midwife holds my hand and coos soothing words in German; the doctor works quickly and I'm on my way home with my husband in half an hour, back at work the next day. My husband says, "You made a brave decision. You are brave . . . considering . . ."

Considering . . .

URANIUM MINERS INHERIT DISPUTE'S
SAD LEGACY

From 1947 until the early 1960s, two Federal agencies struggled in secret over the fate of thousands of men who were being exposed to hazardous levels of radiation while mining uranium for the nuclear weapons industry. . . . The Atomic Energy Commission prevailed in the battle over mine safety with the Public Health Service. The result has been a widening trail of deaths and disabilities from lung cancer across Arizona, Colorado, New Mexico and Utah, according to Federal and state researchers.

New York Times, JANUARY 9, 1990

October 1, 1954. My birthday. My husband is keeping a close watch on me today because I am now thirty years old and he fears I'll—what?—sink into a gloom he can't enter? But I'm feeling fine and am striding beside the Isar, taking in the red leaves falling on a yellow path, the water below gurgling over henna rocks, swirling dry leaves, the cold breeze biting my ears. My figure has returned as though it knew I'd need it, that I would not want to be reminded. I like to use my body for long meandering walks through Munich suburbs, to see the building going on, to run down precipitous paths like a careless sure-footed boy, to bike two miles to Oberwiesenfeld, Hitler's former airport, where my job is located. Much has been planned for this evening—dinner with friends, an Orff opera, dessert—*Prinz Regententorte*—at the new dwelling provided for us by Radio Liberation.

The furnished apartment overlooks the Isar and is not new except to us. An *altbau,* built in the twenties, not bombed. A grand piano, a Blaupunkt short-wave radio, crimson velvet, built-in seats on two sides of the living room, a brass bed in the bedroom.

Germans like to promenade and the path alongside the Isar is a popular locale. Mothers with babies in carriages, old men bundled up in green loden coats, svelte gay men holding hands or throwing dry leaves at each other, one shouting, "*Vorsicht!*"; the other, "Look Out, Idiot!" I'm in a foreign land; I can't remember Berkeley or Princeton. Was that me there, or someone else?

A woman walks beside me, matching my footsteps. I speed up, so does she. I steal a side glance and see a woman wrapped in grays and black, long blonde hair with red mixed in, her eyes focused on the path ahead. I slow down, hoping she'll forge ahead, but she steps in front of me and I stop lest I run into her. The sun has set and light is fading. I should turn around and go home, get ready for our celebratory evening, but when I start to turn away she places her hand on my arm. I say, "Excuse me, but do I know you?"

She takes a deep breath with a squeaky cry buried inside: "We haven't talked in quite a while and I'm not surprised you don't recognize me. I'm Barren Woman."

"Oh yes, of course. But you see I talk with another now, who walks with me. Her name is Woman-Who-

Has-Had-A-Stillbirth. I can't talk to more than one, people would think me daft."

"You need to talk to both of us. We are the same, not two, one."

"No. *She* is not barren!"

"I see we must refer to what you like to call your 'lexicon.' *Barren,* incapable of producing, or not producing, offspring."

"*She* was pregnant; she felt the quickening, she gave birth. She did!"

"Dead. Dead in utero. A malformed skull. In the beginning, a bad egg."

"No! My eggs, this egg, was fine. Something happened; I don't know what, no one knows. Something outside of me, in the environment. A fluke. It won't happen next time."

"Next time, the same odds, but this is not a game of chance. Nature works with what is there and you have told me that you believe that your cluster of eggs was damaged long ago."

"But don't you see that I don't believe that now? I was pregnant, she kicked inside me, I *know* next time will be different. Woman-Who-Has-Had-A-Stillbirth knows this."

"She is a false witness, Candida, a dishonest scientist. She wants your company, wants to walk with you, enjoys seeing you healthy and optimistic. She wants to join your birthday celebration; she likes opera and rich desserts."

"Yes! And you, why don't you jump into the Isar and drown. *She* is my companion now." Forgiving my rudeness, she smiles and runs a cold finger down my cheek. I turn my back and stare down at the trace of last light on the water below. I know she'll return and perhaps my companions will argue with each other and all I'll have to do is listen.

The Fulbright is extended for a second year. My husband researches and writes; I type what he writes and work with émigrés each day. I climb over the high wall of my prejudice and learn to like, even love, the few Germans we mesh into our lives, especially the von Behr family. Hartwig, who broods in his study and rules his wife and children, earnestly adores this American couple and continually tries to settle the question of his guilt or impotence in allowing Hitler to come to power. He wants a soothing answer, but each time my husband gives him a tentative acceptable excuse, he backs up and flays himself all over again from yet another perspective. Regula, his wife, cooks, cares for their two children, will not discuss history or politics, says to me, "Let's take a long *spazier* . . . walk . . . today and I speak the English every moment."

At Oberweisenfeld, there is Eva who has all the American men entranced and eager to date her. She turns them all down with a shake of her head, a blush reddening her neck. As we become friends, I fall into her story gradually, accepting strange facets—she was betrothed to Roland when she was six years old—as though she were a character in a Russian novel. When she was nineteen, she went to England to learn English, fell in love with an English schoolteacher who wants to marry her, memorized sonnets and decided that English is the language of love and that one can't *love* in German. She plays Bach on my piano from memory and Roland does not want her to see me because he thinks an American woman is certainly a bad influence. Once he came to our apartment and demanded that Eva leave with him and go to her own house. She stood in the door and said, "Roland! You behave very bad! Go!" Meanwhile, at work, uncouth Americans from Yale or Harvard go out of their way all day long just to gaze at her lush breasts and tiny waist and chestnut hair curling, escaping her tortoise-shell combs. Green eyes with thick lashes. She tells me her older brother died on the Russian front. When the Americans marched into Munich, she was eleven and she stood out in the street and spat at them. Now she prefers them to Roland but will marry him because she will do as her family has promised. Not to do so would shame them. Roland is a rugby player and goes to Taliesin West to study architecture. He runs away with Frank Lloyd Wright's daughter but Eva doesn't fret: "Candida, I don't *love* Roland, I'm just going to marry with him." One Yalie says to her, "Sweet Eva, if you won't let me take you to dinner, would you just let me *see* your breasts, just once, please?" She asks me what I think she should do. I have no opinion but am very interested in the rest of the story. She agrees and lets him *look* for five minutes, in his apartment, and then she dresses her top part and goes home.

There are three categories of workers at Radio Liberation. Starting at the top, there are American men and their American female staffs. Just below this level, German women do all the "unclassified" clerical work. Tucked into small offices throughout the vast plant are all the stateless émigrés, men who do the actual work of writing and broadcasting to the warring nationalities inside the Soviet Union. Their wives, lovers, sisters and children often ride out on bicycles and wait until the men can go home. The women, in summer, wear embroidered sleeveless blouses cut low over their breasts, billowing skirts and sturdy sandals. I can't understand how they can appear to be so happy, how or why they do impromptu dances while they wait. They greet their men with fierce embraces as though they've just returned from war. They live in hovels, often with no hot water. They raise their slightly plump arms as they jig, and I can see clumps of dark or tawny hair in their armpits. Their legs are strong and hairy, their breasts flop up and down and their nipples show through the thin cloth.

In contrast, the American women and the German clerks wear suits and bras, stockings, heels, and they certainly don't dance at work. Suddenly I begin to understand that the American men are finding the underarm thickets ever so sexy and are studying the hairy legs, trying to make up their minds. I begin to let my armpits sprout, and find that I love the feel of hair there when I move an arm towards my typewriter. These stateless, doomed women are redefining us, loosening our fashion rules, changing the ways in which we approach our men. My husband is instantly converted. And at night, when not at work, the émigré men, while drinking liters of beer and vodka, dance until they drop; they seem to have brought accordions, drums, violins into exile. There's often a party until dawn and then off to work they go. The German female staff watches, their mouths pursed; they like the exotic but prefer it to be across the border in Italy.

I haven't forgotten Mical, Monsanto, Oak Ridge, Hiroshima, but I seem to have assigned worry and sorrow to dreams in which I search for lost kittens through rubble, where Death visits as a clanking skeleton with a child held in his arms. When I awake crying, my husband holds me, says, "There, there." I have been inhabiting a pleasant intermission, but he has steadily piled up the research that will lead to a PhD, and at the start of the coldest winter in Munich's history, in December 1955, he returns to the United

States to seek a position as assistant professor with dissertation almost written. As sole provider of funds, I remain in Munich. Christmas Eve I spend with Eva's family and see a Christmas tree laden with lighted candles and real oranges; I hear German carols on the street outside their house, we pray to the Virgin for a future healthy baby, Eva plays the Coffee Cantata on the piano, her mother kisses and hugs me. On Christmas Day I bicycle to the von Behrs' and receive similar treatment. I know that soon I'll have to leave Munich and I don't want to go. I want to forever cycle to the opera several nights a week, paying twenty-five cents for a ticket, see Munch and Nolde in galleries, sleep in a brass bed, fall off my bike onto the ice, defy the police, laugh at Picasso and be shushed by serious German gallery viewers. I've been enjoying my life as conquering visitor, language deprived, and thus not receiving the profound worries, sorrow, regrets of the residents who shiver outside the markets and hold out tin cups for a few pfennigs.

In April, the good news comes by telephone (downstairs in the entryway of the apartment)—his assignment is Barnard College and we'll be living in New York City. "Come home right away. I miss you ferociously! Don't cut your hair, promise? And don't come home by way of London. Ask the Committee to pack for you and tell them to be careful of my books. Kiss Eva and all the von Behrs for me and don't *delay.* I miss you!"

Tucked under the telephone are two letters from Berkeley:

Dear dear friend—I have delayed writing so long after your sad announcement because . . . our beloved Willi, the very center of our lives for four short years, died a year ago of a brain tumor. One day he was well, the next day he screamed when I ran the vacuum, a few days later he slipped into a coma and was gone. His father said no, no, no, and drank, even holding his classes while drunk. I said yes and when I next see you, this summer I hope, our second child will have been delivered to the battered couple who have lost their innocence. Though hard, it's the only way to be halfway sane. In fall, we take up duties at Ohio

State and I'll not be sad to leave this town of sorrow.

Love you, as always,

Marg

and

Dear daughter,

The other evening your Ex paid a call on us, bringing with him his wife and infant son. He asked about you and was sorry to hear . . . Your husband hints that perhaps you'll visit this summer before he starts work at Barnard. I hope so. It's been almost three years, too too long away.

Your loving father

On the one hand, good news. A respectable job (position), a husband who wants me to hurry to him, my life resuming its customary torments. On the other hand, a child can die suddenly, his soft pink cheeks cold, his black eyes closed. I want to stay with this picture but the news about my Ex lurks. The baby . . . did his sperm revive? Need I know? Perhaps my eggs, cozy in my dark interior, have repaired themselves since evicting their defective member. I wish I could pull each egg into the light and when they all sit around me on the carpet, ask each one, "How do you feel? Healthy? Vigorous? *Normal?*" If the answer wavers, that egg would not be able to return. It would shrivel and dry up at my feet.

On page one I was eight years old, sitting high in a eucalyptus tree. That was my viewpoint and my point of view was that of an eight-year-old. The tense was present—"There's a breeze . . ."—and nothing happened except in my head, my remembered, recalled, invented head.

Pages followed, and each time there was a point of view, often a physical viewpoint. This is called "memoir" and the term insists that I have indeed remembered what I have written. However, I cannot simply print out thoughts from the head of an eight-year-old up a tree. I have also invented. By calling it *memoir,* I require that you believe my words, my memory, and forget that it is an invention, an edifice of thought.

When I left Candida the year was 1956 and she was thirty-one. She was slowly—in first person, present tense—trudging through the years, and she'll continue advancing towards us, but at a much faster pace now. I must accelerate her dogged pursuit of information about her egg pouch because I have been arm-wrestling with Mother Mortality: a chaotic thyroid, a raging pulse, a rock-and-roll heartbeat. Slowly we matched our strengths, and I could remember my telephone number again and could begin to think of a few words to type on white paper.

It seems like a reward for surviving when my government kisses the top of my head. I even think we may hug, them 'n' me, enemies over the decades. My government reaches me on January 29 beneath "All The News That's Fit to Print" in the upper left corner of the first page of the *New York Times,* in caps:

U.S. ACKNOWLEDGES RADIATION
KILLED WEAPONS WORKERS
ENDS DECADES OF DENIALS
Compensation is Possible for Survivors of Cancer
Victims Who Worked on Bombs

After decades of denials, the government is conceding that since the dawn of the atomic age, workers making nuclear weapons have been exposed to radiation and chemicals that have produced cancer and early death.

President Clinton ordered the study in July. . . . The president asked for a broad study that would look at the effects of radiation and chemical hazards from uranium, plutonium and other substances.

Of the new conclusion, Energy Secretary Bill Richardson said in an interview, "This is the first time that the government is acknowledging that people got cancer from radiation exposure in the plants. . . . In the past, the role of government was to take a hike, and I think that was wrong."

The draft report says that in addition to several other operations at Oak Ridge, Tenn., where K-25 was situated, elevated cancer levels were found at Savannah River in South Carolina and Hanford in eastern Washington State, where plutonium was manufactured; at Rocky Flats near Denver, where plutonium was shaped into weapons components; at the Fernald Feed Materials Center near Cincinatti, where uranium was processed, and at the Lawrence Livermore and Los Alamos national laboratories.

In the months before the *New York Times* article there is a book I take with me wherever I go—in the car, out to dinner, on walks with my dog. I clutch it lovingly to my chest and gaze down at the alluring yellow Post-its leaking from its pages, each one marking a nuclear crime inside. The cover is shiny gray, and the title is in raised, white capitals that I can read with my finger like braille: *The Plutonium Files: America's Secret Medical Experiments in the Cold War.* Five hundred eighty pages, $26.95. Dial Press.

No one encourages me, or even allows me to read excerpts while they eat their salmon and Caesar salads. They say, "We already *know.* We don't want to hear more about that! Put the book away and enjoy your dinner." But they don't know; they excuse themselves by saying "Everyone knows the government lies, lied and will lie. You're off on your conspiracy trek again. Who's the author? Another nut?"

"The author," I say, "is a woman named Eileen Welsome, and she's a Pulitzer Prize winner—1994, for investigative reporting for the *Albuquerque Tribune*. This book reveals *fifty years* of lying, of harm to people. I want you to care and to ask why."

"Why? Why did they lie? Keep it short because you haven't even lifted your fork. No, don't tell us now. Pass the book on to us when you've finished and we'll look at it, maybe even read it."

THE WOMAN IS THERE in Munich in 1956 and she has to get to here in California in 2000. I'm ready now to be seventy-five years old and look back at her. I'll be pushing, wanting her to hurry. I'll ask more penetrating questions, saying to her, Don't you remember what you did next? You say you won't remember those years? Well I do, perhaps not every detail, but enough of the story to get you to 1958, 1960, then the fast years until 1978 when you sat down to write one story or another. People died; you can name them and what killed them. I'll take you to the places where they died. It wasn't old age. Sometimes it was disease that ate their innards so fast we scarcely had time to notice they were sick.

Our government has opened one dark closet and will open more and more interiors, and we can now move more swiftly with our words, the air filling our lungs, good air stamped with the government's seal of approval.

The fallout from the bomb tests drifted down over the Earth. The radioactive debris found its way into starfish, shellfish, and seaweed. It covered alfalfa fields in upstate New York, wheat fields in North Dakota, corn in Iowa. It seeped into the bodies of honeybees and birds, human fetuses and growing children. The atom has split the world into "pre-atomic" and "post-atomic" species.

. . . In the summer of 1953, as the radioactive debris from the Upshot-Knothole test gusted across the continent, a group of military and civilian scientists convened at the RAND Corporation headquarters in Santa Monica, California. . . . The group decided the only way they could properly ascertain worldwide hazards from fallout was by collecting and analyzing plants, animals, and human tissue, one of the most bizarre and ghoulish projects of the Cold War. The source of its name [Operation Sunshine] is a matter of debate, but some say it was derived from the fact that fallout, like sunshine, covered the globe.

. . . According to a 1995 General Accounting Office study, Operation Sunshine was the largest of fifty-nine "tissue analysis studies" conducted by atomic scientists during the Cold War. Collectively, the body parts of more than 15,000 humans were used in those studies. In countless instances, scientists took the corpses and organs of deceased people without getting permission from the next of kin.

For Operation Sunshine alone, approximately 9,000 samples of human bones, entire skeletons, and nearly 600 human fetuses were collected from around the world. Since the project was initially classified *Secret,* researchers concocted "cover stories" that they used in order to acquire human samples from abroad.

EILEEN WELSOME, *THE PLUTONIUM FILES,* pages 299–300

Mical, you were born in Munich in March 1954. Were you "collected"?

1956

LONDON AND BOW BRICKHILL

WEAPONS PLANT IS PRESSED FOR DETAILS
OF TOLL ON HEALTH

Denver, the Rocky Flats Plant, the sole supplier of plutonium triggers for thermonuclear weapons, is facing the most intense pressure in its 38-year history for a full public accounting of accidents and operations that have contaminated the Denver area with plutonium. "I've always found that when you talk about Rocky Flats in this area, everybody has just a piece of the truth," said Albert J. Hazle, a radiation protection specialist for the Colorado Department of Health. "The environmentalists have a piece. People living around the plant have a piece. The state has a piece. . . . It's time for the Energy Department to make the whole truth known."

The New York Times, FEBRUARY 15, 1990

In 1956, I return to the United States by way of London in spite of my husband's urgent telegram. Our friend Anthony Harvey has invited me to visit on my way home; I shall stay at his home with his father and sister and let him show me his hometown. Anthony is a classics scholar who spent laughing time with us in Munich while studying the violin. We traveled with him to Lake Como and Switzerland. He is veddy English and just the sort of guide I need, yet so innocent that I am embarrassed my husband doesn't trust us together. I hope he doesn't find out.

I arrive on May 1 and find London in bloom with annuals in window boxes, fruit trees in pink blossom, pedestrians strolling down the busy streets, often stopping on the sidewalk to lift their pale faces to the sun. We ride in his Morris Minor at an insane speed directly to his home in Kensington, where his father and sister join us for lunch. Anthony can't stop smiling; he is so pleased to be host to an American friend. His father, very handsome, is a Queen's Counsel, and when the rickety cage elevator groans to a stop on the top floor, there is Mr. Harvey murmuring soft greetings, leading us into the flat, telling us lunch will be served in "hof" an hour. He asks how was my journey "cross channel" and do I want milk with my meal, which "all Americans insanely like," or tea?

At lunch, Anthony's sister Jean joins us using a walker and approaching slowly slowly down the long hallway. She is in her mid-twenties and was felled by polio while doing relief work in Holland after the war. After she allows Anthony to push her chair up to the table and then bows her head as he says grace, I remember that on our visits with Anthony to Lake Como, we would find him each morning sitting in the sun writing a letter either to his mother, who was dying of cancer, or to his sister, who was trying to learn to walk again. This family seems indefinably different from any family I've ever known. Is it their dignity? Their courage? Their stiff upper lips? Their refusal to recite calamity? I have the sudden feeling, there in the sunny dining room, that what they have is something I shall never have, that their approach to living is sealed in their past, centuries of upright behavior, of assigning complaint and whinging to a category of weakness they rule out. I sit up straighter and sip my tea.

Oh, the nine days are full, and there are no telegrams. Sun, every day. I accompany Anthony to the BBC, where he works and is preparing a broadcast about America's most famous poet, Emily. I listen to the recorded poems and shyly offer the opinion that her poems sound a bit off in an English accent. Before I can object or practice I am taping the same poems in my own voice. I visit Mr. Harvey in his chambers and watch him listen to testimony in a white wig. I go to a party Anthony's staff is giving and find it odd that I am the only woman there. Don't these men have wives? I ask. Anthony looks puzzled and says, "I don't know. Should I know?" We visit Jean's handicrafts-by-the-handicapped "shoppe" in London. I buy note-paper painted by an artist whose hands were blown off in the war. We go to a grand performance of twelve harpsichords at the Royal Festival Hall that honors the maker of these instruments. Anthony plays on stage and later tells me that Oh yes, he also has a clavichord and a flute and a recorder. Twelve harpsichords playing Bach together must be the sound of heaven if there is a heaven.

Each night I sleep in the guest room with a hot

water bottle at my feet and lavender-scented sheets wrapped up close to my nose. For three days we stay at the Harveys' country house twenty miles distant from London's noise and pace. Bow Brickhill they call it. Again the lavender but heated bricks at the foot of my bead instead of a hot water bottle. Mr. Harvey climbs a ladder on the side of the cottage to remove a pest starling's nest and then is very upset when he drops an egg and it smashes on the stones below. He announces at dinner that Anthony will train to become a minister, and that seems to him to be a terrible waste of his son's education. I have never heard his son say one word about God. But why would he, in the presence of barbarian Americans?

Anthony and I walk on the heath, go through turnstiles, sit on a low fence and look out at the heather and bracken. And we discuss the "efficacy" of prayer. I fancy I'm on Wuthering Heights on a spring day. I seem powered by new synapses, since I don't know what "efficacy" means and have never prayed. At sunset we all walk up to the little church on the hill as the church bells ring, and Anthony plays Handel on the organ and parishioners call him Master Anthony.

Mr. Harvey bows his head in prayer, then sinks down on his knees and says softly, "No, no, no."

I want a new nationality, want to stay in England, feel I have new skin but know it is an enchantment, perhaps intended to encourage me in my return to my husband. At the dock before I board the *Queen Elizabeth,* I hug my host and weep a few tears. "Don't try so hard," he says. "Just be good to each other." There is honey in his words.

1956

PRINCETON AND BERKELEY

GROWING UP AS A NUCLEAR GUINEA PIG

BY TOM TAILIE

Mesa, Wash. The exposure began the same day our lives began. . . . During my childhood I remember seeing men dressed in space suits walking in front of uniformed soldiers carrying shovels and sacks. . . . They brought us candy and, one time, cowboy boots. What we didn't know at the time was that these were nuclear clean-up crews. . . . I was born a year after my stillborn brother. I struggled to breathe through under-developed lungs, and suffered to overcome numerous birth defects. I underwent multiple surgeries, endured paralysis, thyroid medication, a stint in an iron lung, loss of hair, sores over my body, fevers, poor hearing, asthma, teeth rotting out and, at age 18, a diagnosis of sterility. . . . Who the hell do these people in the nuclear gang think they are? . . . The world now knows about Hanford's releases. We were the children on the front lines in the cold war. . . . Moscow was condemned for its three days of silence after the Chernobyl nuclear accident. What about Washington's 40 years of silence?

The New York Times, JULY 22, 1990

The reunion in Princeton is sweet, and again we mate and mate on a bed, in a house turned over to us by a vacationing professor. Our apartment in New York, subsidized by Columbia University, will not be available until early September. Late May, it is already hot and humid and I can't seem to take into my body enough air to propel me through each day. Princeton, in all seasons, is attractive, but in summer it yields and bows to plant growth and the vines seem to be reaching out to strangle, wrap, trip. Every day, in late afternoon, it rains, sometimes hails, with lightning illuminating the graduate student tower. The house has no air-conditioning, and my daily task is to type my husband's most recent pages after he departs for his carrel in the library. His career, our future, wife. It seems much too soon to be back in harness, and indeed the life I have reentered doesn't fit. Why are several marginally attractive faculty wives leaving casseroles on our doorstep every other day? Why is there one pearl earring in the medicine cabinet? Why do the pages I am typing seem *in medias res* instead of leading towards a conclusion of his research? Isn't he supposed to show up at Barnard with dissertation finished?

At night, in the hot bedroom with the fan roaring, I lie back and dream of the Isar, biking to the opera, the yellow marigolds surrounding Anthony's mother's grave at Bow Brickhill. I feel the shudder of the pew seat when Anthony sounds the last chord of Handel. Since my first moment back at Princeton, I have felt covered by damp gauze, a film over my eyes making it difficult to see across the living room or decipher a house number I'm seeking. A few friends, noticing that I am unusually somber, ask if I am experiencing "culture shock." This idea is new to me and it percolates. I am certain it isn't German, Bavarian, European culture I am missing. For three years I have been free to partake or reject, to mock their laws or comply if to my advantage. Waving my American passport, I could ride my bike on their pedestrian paths, lie on forbidden grass, wear sneakers when pregnant. Now, suddenly, my harness chafes, my feet feel bound, the heavy air of Princeton that I had thought at fault morphs into wife culture, academic-expectations culture, career-path culture, type-all-day-drink-gin-and-tonics-with-friends-until-bedtime culture.

At breakfast, on another scorching morning with my hands around a glass of iced coffee, I say, "As usual, the hot weather is making me ill and I think I should go to Berkeley to see my parents whom I've not seen since . . . is that 'whom' or 'who'? . . . since . . . well, for three years or more, and get a clerical job there for the summer months and earn enough to fly back in the fall and you could go too and work on your dissertation at UC's library and we'd see old friends and be *comfortable* and I'm sure someone will have a car we can borrow if we want to go to the mountains on a weekend and the rest of the time we can walk or take buses . . ."

"Where will we live? Certainly not with your parents."

"Oh, a sublet close to the campus. Somewhere. I

could go soon, maybe in a few days, and find us a place. . . ."

A week later, in a plane over Ohio, it occurs to me to worry that he has no intention of joining me in Berkeley, that this is the end for us, a fade-out without ugly quarrel. I stare at my left hand with the gold band on the ring finger, move the finger so that light catches the gold. I feel sad but in my head "So be it" keeps sounding so insistent that I think the person sitting next to me can surely hear the words. I recall his sweaty face at the airport, his damp strong hug, his jaunty "See you soon!" as I entered the tunnel into the plane. I close my eyes and dream of the Isar again, and when I wake we are descending and the ocean is blue down below and I can see all the ticky-tacky houses in South San Francisco that once I'd thought ugly but sparkle now in the sun and are ever so charming.

IN TEN DAYS, with oxygen coursing through my blood, the cool sun inviting me out on errands, I start typing a dissertation for pay, find a small sublet available immediately, babble Munich stories at my parents and find out that not only will my father not listen, he mournfully leaves the room if I even hint that some of the Germans are quite nice. Or he walks over to the TV and turns it on, draws up a stool and sits with his back to me. He has always been a source of historical information for me, and I find it disturbing that he will not open his mind on Germany. He could now teach me, and for the first time in my life he is refusing. I wonder if he is a bit senile, or whether I was under a spell over there.

I hike up the hill to visit Glo and Marty (the carpenter/contractor). They are not overly friendly but answer my bald questions: "Did they have any trouble getting pregnant?" I of course am not referring to Glo and Marty, who definitely do not want children. They know I mean my ex-husband. Glo says no, right away she was pregnant, no difficulty at all. The happy family is right across the street; perhaps I should visit if I am asking questions about them. They offer that the young mother of two darling girls in the house above on the ridge suddenly died of malignant melanoma and I say I already know that. They do not ask questions about Germany and seem eager for me to end the visit. My feet are heavy as bricks as I walk back down the hill.

The next morning I have an appointment with Dr. G., who pronounces me fit and does not duck when I ask him why, why a malformed skull. He says he doesn't know, it could be this or that; perhaps it was an "insulted baby," a baby harmed early in the pregnancy by lack of enough oxygen in the hot, Princeton summer. Isn't that a fine term—insulted baby—worth a poem?

WHEN MY HUSBAND ARRIVES in early July—pleased to be out of the heat, ready to spill Germany stories to anyone who will listen, amorous, optimistic about our future, I carefully keep from him all knowledge of my yearning to fix the cause of my (our) stillborn child. He would sympathize, but sympathy would not have rid me of my quiet obsession. No, I have to be sneaky, question people when he is elsewhere, check books out of the library—books about levels of radiation in different parts of the country. But I leave them at work, or read them on a park bench, then return them to the library. I believe that if he knows, for instance, that when I say I am going for a walk but hike up the hill to the Lawrence Radiation Lab and sit on a curb across from a locked gate and stare at people leaving and entering, even imagine clouds of radiation floating over the fence, he will place me firmly in a category of people, some of them beloved, who are "off," twisted by an experience in life that doesn't yield to analysis, who must be humored and protected until well again or until life shows another face. Our little girl, Mical, is not for him a little girl who did not live long enough to get born. She was a grisly organic mess that fortunately was not born alive, requiring us to care for her in her helplessness until we hated her and each other.

The summer is fleet and pleasant, filled with home-cooked dinners, happy guests, renewals of friendships, visits to couples who have become parents during the three years we were away ("so sorry for your loss"), detailed analyses of situations where a couple has split and united with others, or hasn't and the one left behind is bitter or grieves.

One evening my husband says he will cook dinner and we shall invite my parents, my sister, two of his aunts and several friends. He is not a cook; I've never known him even to boil an egg. He is a talented talker, a teller of shaggy-dog stories. I don't recall the full menu, but one item is oven-baked stuffed mush-rooms, which he begins to prepare at about seven-thirty, though he knows my parents always eat at six. I make a fine salad with shrimp, baby tomatoes, spinach leaves, tender young lettuce and anchovies. We all drink gin-and-tonics, and talk. Talk. Talk. Eight o-clock, eight-thirty, on towards nine. My father is stiffening, about to erupt; my mother is almost passed out on the couch. She is not a drinker. I am on my best behavior and don't want to nag because I hope he will consent to try for a baby again in the fall. Soon, he says, fifteen minutes in the oven.

At 9:45 he pulls the tray of mushrooms from the oven, puts three or four shriveled specimens on each plate. I toss the salad together, mix the dressing in with my hands, drop a shiny portion beside the mush-rooms, begin passing this very late dinner to each guest. Long before everyone is served my father blows. "CHRIST! This is some kind of cruel joke, isn't it? Sand in the mushrooms, or whatever these black things are, pebbles, tiny ones! I should have known that a scholar can't do two things at the same time! Disgusting, I'm going home." While other guests look down at their plates, take cautious bites, spit them out, my sister says quietly, "I believe you forgot to cook the rice before stuffing it into the mushrooms, right?" My father exits, with my mother in tow saying, "Now dear, don't be cruel," and he is saying "Goddam idiot!" The other guests, giddy with gin, are appreciating the salad, and my husband, after looking stunned, bewildered, sheepish, already begins forming the tale of the night he fixed dinner for his in-laws and forgot to cook the rice. Even prim Aunt Bess almost falls out of her chair laughing.

Aunt Bess and Aunt Edie are my husband's Jewish aunts, on his mother's side. Bess is a stylish San Francisco widow who keeps herself busy with various philanthropic duties—opera, orphans, city planning. She lives alone at the corner of Divisidero and Green streets in a flat with a view of the Palace of Fine Arts and San Francisco Bay. Edie is also a widow, who lives alone in Berkeley and has worked for many years at UC Berkeley researching the nature of the child. Both aunts are well read, fast talking, no-nonsense women who have opinions not easily altered by an upstart nephew. At the close of the late-dinner evening, Edie says, "You really should go see your cousin in the country, but do *not* talk about Germany. I think you understand."

THE WEEKEND BEFORE WE RETURN to the east coast, driving north to Sebastopol to visit Edie's son Ken, his wife, Ann, and their child, I debate with myself whether to ask my husband if he *does* understand that Ken, imprisoned in a wheelchair, shot down over Germany in the war, once a vigorous athlete, might not want to hear about Germany, not even from his dear cousin whose second field of scholarly study is Nazi history, myth and fact. Deciding that Edie's words are warning enough, I drift into wondering how Ken and Ann had conceived a child and wish I could ask but know I can't. Why are such interesting subjects *verboten,* and why is that German word so ominous and the word "forbidden" not the least?

Their spacious country house with the oak-studded hills in the distance, the two golden retrievers bringing balls to us, the yellow-haired toddler hanging on their necks, dogs rolling on the grass in their front yard, even the concrete ramp circling up to the front door, all this is studiedly cheerful. Ken's strong brown arms hug my husband's neck and they laugh and sock each other, fists withholding force, extending affection, recalling a former time when they wrestled without restraint. Ann and I move off to look at the flowers—geranium red, bougainvillea crimson—and the pool she says Ken uses daily to ease his pain. She says it simply, without further comment.

A middle-aged woman who seems to be a servant brings sandwiches to the pool area, and it is while we are eating, and drinking glasses of white wine, that I notice my husband and Ken are not talking to each other, most unusual in such a yakky family. I am sitting on the grass, the child by my side, when Ken in his wheelchair above me throws his sandwich on the tile, begins a keening "I'LL NEVER FORGET," aims the chair at my husband, screeches, "HOW COULD YOU COME TO MY HOUSE AND SAY THERE'S GOOD ONES, BAD ONES AND IN-BETWEENS, THAT WE HAVE TO TRY TO

UNDERSTAND, GET OUT GET OUT," and then he tries to rise from his chair and crashes to the ground. As I rush to try to help, I see saliva glistening on his lips, red and swollen with fury. The child is crying; Ann is lifting Ken, the servant helping. My husband takes my hand and we walk slowly to our car. "I didn't, I wasn't . . . ," he says. "I know," I say. "I think I know, it was not possible . . . he didn't want . . . he couldn't . . ." We give up on words and for the first time in our life with each other, we find nothing to say all the way back to Berkeley.

My husband flies east in the middle of September. The New York apartment is ready for occupancy. Furniture, bookshelves, household equipment have to be scrounged from Goodwill or from friends. Pages are waiting to be typed. I have to seek a part-time job on campus, look into ways of obtaining a quick New York teaching credential, and the apartment really needs to be painted any color to cover the green he calls "snot green." The pattern of our relocating is that he goes on ahead across a continent or an ocean, views the lay of the land, and then I follow, often reluctantly, not because I don't want to be with him (I tell myself), but because once there, at his side,

I become his typist, his cook, his painter, his researcher, his shopper, his lay, and it is much more fun delaying all of those duties, postponing in the fall sun of my hometown the wife accretions of these years. Once I am in gear, I find it impossible to locate the self so vividly present to me in Berkeley.

Berkeley is patterned with locales that speak to me, say "Remember when . . . ?" When I walk again to the Radiation Lab I recall living down the street from Ernest O. Lawrence on Tamalpais Road and hear my father saying, "Oh God, the Nobel Prize winner, that smiling fathead!" And then I walk up that street and remember my bratty brother (eight years younger), who entered with his sidekicks the house of Lawrence and wrote "Fuck" in red lipstick on the mirror of little Mary Lawrence's bedroom, lied, then confessed, and the shame I felt. I walk in the Rose Garden and can smell the Lysol of my sailor date's uniform blending with the perfume of the roses, feel the sad apprehension, the knowing that this young man might not come back, that I wouldn't even know because he is from Red Wing, Minnesota, and his name would not be listed in the *Berkeley Gazette* as

missing or dead. Walking on Shattuck Avenue, headed
in the direction of Berkeley High, I remember the
pink baby rose pinned to my hair, the white angora
bobby socks fuzzing above white buck shoes, the moment Lizanne and I would pause, say "Ready?" and
race the last block, zipping into class at the last allow-
able moment, sweaty, giggling. She always won by
at least twenty feet. Climbing the hills, I spot the
dwellings vacated by our Japanese friends in 1941 and
wish I knew more certainly that they survived. I am
not happy in Berkeley; that isn't the point. I am alive
and am sure I won't be in Manhattan. When I tell
him my fears by phone, he says that he and I will im-
print Manhattan with our thoughts, our footsteps,
our feasting with friends, our alluring presence in the
greatest of American cities. But I know he will take
root; I will float, lose form and definition, fade.

In the week I lag behind, I chat with the residents
on the road up to my ex-husband's house and discover
that Janet, who had lived "downwind," has had a radical
mastectomy and returned to Brooklyn with her husband. "Downwind" is a word we understand and use
now, always with a shiver of fear; then, I would have

said that Janet lived "above the cyclotron" and would have silently tested the theory that we might, just possibly, be passive guinea pigs. I remember that Janet had helped us water the roofs of houses one hot September day; we feared a small blaze near the lab might spread the fumes, the poisons from burning poison oak. My ex-husband had growled to me while spraying our roof, "Lawrence thought the cyclotron should be built in an uninhabited area because that was safer. He knew a big cyclotron would send out radiation." We were "upwind" and he was the only person well enough informed to utter the word "radiation." His mouth, so long shut by army command, was opening.

THE NEW YORK TIMES, November 7, 1993:

SOVIET ATOMIC BOMB TEST EXPOSED 45,000 TO HIGH LEVEL OF RADIATION

Humans Were Guinea Pigs in Russia Atomic Tests, Archives Show. It's on Film

In August, Yuri Sorokin, an intelligence officer who took part in the Totskoye exercise, filed suit in

Moscow against the Russian Ministry of Defense, the first case of its kind. He is asking for the equivalent of $52,000 for his suffering, including undefined diseases affecting his heart, head, stomach and lungs. He is convinced the military knew what it was doing; on the way to Totskoye, he told reporters, some of his comrades noticed train cars filled with new coffins.

1957-58
MANHATTAN, BERKELEY

*Time can be measured in many ways. . . . Now, in
my mind, I can feel myself moving backward in
time. I am as if on a train. And the train pushes into
history. This history seems to exist somewhere,
waiting, a foreign country behind a border and,
perhaps also inside me.*

SUSAN GRIFFIN, *A CHORUS OF STONES*, page 114

I am living in Manhattan, half a block from Columbia University, a block from Barnard, six blocks
from Harlem. I attend Bergman films at the Thalia
Theater with lively, erudite companions. I take the

bus to the Metropolitan and view Renoirs and Van Goghs. I paint our apartment red, yellow and blue; nubile girls follow my husband and me whenever we walk across the quad. Late at night there are screams and gunshot sounds and St. Luke's Hospital, in the next block, receives whining ambulances. I shop at Gristede's, half a block away and, with packages in my arms, return home and climb to the third floor. I fear the dark corners of the stairwell and am not surprised when winter arrives and I must step over a dead body in front of our building.

Mornings I work for Professor Otto Klineberg, sorting his mail, rearranging his files. He is never in his office. Sylvia Knopf stops by my desk every day to tell me what her analyst said to her yesterday, then what she said and what her boyfriend said and did, and the psychologists down the hall torture rabbits and rats in their cages. One of my husband's students at Barnard is a brilliant poet and another gives me a hardback copy of *The Second Sex,* by Simone de Beauvoir and I hope it will never end.

Time, however, in 1956 and part of 1957, when I am thirty-two and thirty-three, is not measured by films, art, gifts, grocery shopping, a job. No, not even by the couplings in the dark bedroom whose window opens six inches from a concrete wall, letting in the oily, stinging fuel deposits of passing jets.

I measure time as I count the days past expected menstruation, as I feel and wonder if I am imagining mild soreness of breasts, a sudden dislike of coffee, of my husband's cigarette smell. I won't tell him; I will wait until a month has passed, then two months, and by then he may have noticed a slight increase in the size of my breasts, and I will cross my fingers and allow myself to hope. I feel sick each morning; I vomit and am glad.

Two and a half months and one morning, upon awakening, I become aware of a slight bubble in my vagina and when I pee the toilet water turns pink. Pink, at first, yet by day's end clots of red blood, adhering in the shape of sunny-side-up egg yolk, but red. Red. The nurse at the doctor's office says there is nothing to be done; I will go on bleeding or I will stop. I am probably miscarrying and this is nature's way of ridding itself of material that "cannot go to term."

At 5:00 P.M., I talk again to the nurse. She says, "You are, of course, inspecting the discharge?"

"Inspecting?"

"Yes, I'm sure the doctor told you that if the miscarriage does not complete itself naturally, you will have to have a D and C. But we must be sure that fetal tissue is ejected. If tissue stays inside . . . well, you must inspect.

"How?"

"Each clump of material, probe it. Scoop it out of the toilet bowl and feel it for tissue. Wrap the tissue in wax paper and place it in the refrigerator. Keep doing this until the bleeding tapers off and you begin to feel better. Then make an appointment and bring the tissue to us and we'll determine if the abortion—that's the medical term—has taken place without incident."

"And if it hasn't?"

"We'll see you day after tomorrow at 1:00 P.M. Until then, rest and sleep."

My husband brings me hot milk and whiskey and holds me in his strong arms until I sleep. The pain continues to measure time; with each increase the day slows until I wonder if this measure of time will last forever. The doctor tells me to meet him at Beekman Downtown Hospital with fetal tissue in hand. Doubled over in a wheelchair, I wait while they, in their turn, inspect the contents of the wax paper. Pink gristle, like fat removed from a juicy lamb chop.

It will be years before I am curious enough to question this sequence of events. I believed the doctor, the nurse, the hospital, all were concerned for my health. Perhaps it was Adrienne Rich in *Of Woman Born* or Phyllis Chesler in *Women and Madness* who spelled out for me that by law in New York and elsewhere I could not be scoured of toxic fetal material that might kill me until I provided evidence that a *natural* miscarriage was well on its way.

There are two more miscarriages that year, and on the West Coast, Glo, the carpenter's wife, loses a breast, explodes a disc and now walks with a walker. The carpenter's brother is confined to a wheelchair and is blind in one eye. My parents somehow learn this while walking on the hill.

I try to remember the West Coast, my sister and parents. They are not an integral part of me now. I am silent, invisible, slipping down below the horizon.

IN THE SECOND WEEK OF DECEMBER 1957, I
am once again heavy with an awareness, a lurking nau-
sea, that makes me irritable and gloomy. In this condition, I take the bus to a hotel in lower Manhattan that
is hosting the annual meeting of my husband's historical society. I am invited to the cocktail party that
closes the conference but have declined. I will surprise him. I am wearing a simple, black wool dress,
pointy-toed Italian pumps, my hair freshly washed,
dangling gold earrings. Red, bold lipstick. The weather
is unseasonably mild and I carry my unfashionable
all-weather coat over one arm.

There he is, in the lobby, bent over a charming,
blond, impossibly young woman who is smiling up
into his face, his dark eyes, and he places his hand
gently under her chin. I am a stalking statue, unable to
go forward or backward. My feet are stones. He turns,
recognizes me, steers her forward to greet me, intro-
duces her (a grad student), kisses the top of my head,
offers to bring me a drink. As the grad student backs
away, I ask where the restroom is and he leads me
there, his hand on my elbow. I say, "I'm about to

throw up, but this one is going to hang on, get born, be perfect. I know. A girl."

TIME NOW GOES FORWARD and is measured by fetal changes, the quickening, the kicks, the pulse of another's beating heart. The calendar is marked with these events and all progress heads toward the due date. A purchase of diapers is as momentous and forward-marching as the leaves appearing suddenly on the small tree in front of our building.

In 1958, niched between the anniversary of Hiroshima, August 6, and Nagasaki, August 9, our daughter Emily is born in Berkeley. If our dates are right, and we are sure, she is a ten-month baby. A ten-month baby is not common, but, unlike a "postmature baby," is not in the range of pathology. Dr. G. says before her birth, "When the cherry is ripe, it will fall from the tree." He correctly predicts the gender, the weight at birth, and the time of delivery. She can hold up her head and look around as soon as she arrives. Like her mother, she worries and is anxious. I tell her there is nothing to fear, much to give joy—colors, flowers, sky, ocean, sand, milk, walking, climbing, waking up, sleeping. As a mother, I practice dissembling and almost convince myself.

Yet know this. Since August 1945, when news of both Hiroshima and Nagasaki crawled out from the radios, triumphant or hushed preacher voices, circus-barker brag, presidential pride tinged with doubt, followed by national and international commentary—I have been afraid. Suspicious. I have believed no one, have doubted the yellow in the daffodil, the white of a summer cloud against apparently innocent blue.

With little fanfare and no input from the public, the Nevada site was approved for bomb tests by President Truman in December 1950.

The Atomic Energy Commission embarked upon a highly sophisticated public relations campaign approved by the National Security Council—to gain public acceptance for the tests. The whole thrust of the PR program, according to one memo, was "to make the atom routine in the continental United States and make the public feel at home with atomic blasts and radiation hazards."

Two series of atmospheric tests were conducted in Nevada in 1951. Subsequently, one atmospheric test series per year was conducted in Nevada in 1952, 1953, 1955, 1958, and 1962. Atmospheric tests were conducted in the Pacific in 1946, 1948, 1951, 1952, 1956, 1958, and 1962. In addition, a thirty-kiloton bomb was exploded under water off the coast of San Diego, California in 1955, during Operation Wigwam, and three bombs, ranging from one to two kilotons, were detonated at and near the test site, as well as in Alaska, Colorado, New Mexico, and Mississippi as part of the Plowshare Program, a project aimed at investigating the peaceful uses of nuclear explosives.

Hundreds of downwind residents suffered from both external and internal beta burns caused by fallout during the testing period. AEC investigators later attributed the complaints to "sunburns," "gastro-intestinal disturbance," "hysteria," and "hypothyroidism."

EILEEN WELSOME, *THE PLUTONIUM FILES*, pages 246-247

THE NEW YORK TIMES, January 13, 1994:

· DOCTORS OF DEATH

BY GREG HARKEN AND JAMES DAVID

Report of government radiation experiments on unwitting Americans during the cold war, though shocking, have overlooked an important and sinister element. Some of the plutonium injections and X-rays were performed not only for medical research but also to study potential military applications of radiological poisons. The doctors who carried out some of the experiments were interested not only in saving lives but in taking them.

1958–60

MANHATTAN AND
MIDDLETOWN, CONNECTICUT

US ACKNOWLEDGES RADIATION
KILLED WEAPONS WORKERS
ENDS DECADES OF DENIALS

Compensation Possible for Survivors of Cancer Victims
Who Worked on Bombs

Oak Ridge, Savannah River, Hanford, Rocky Flats,
Lawrence Livermore and Los Alamos.

Cancers were found among nearly 600,000 people who have worked in nuclear weapons production since the start of World War II. They range from leukemia and Hodgkin's lymphoma to cancer of the prostate, kidney, salivary gland and lung.

The New York Times, JANUARY 29, 2000

Still afraid, suspicious, doubting. But when, in the morning light, I gaze at my daughter's face, her somber, brown eyes, her reddish-brown hair, and when she bestows a smile, a chortle, and lifts her arms to me, those unhealthy adjectives vanish as though I have blown my strong breath at a dandelion cluster. We call her Queen Crosspatch because she is seldom contented for long. A stubbled wreck of a man leans over the side of her pram in Manhattan, and when she trembles her chin and starts to cry, he looks at me, saliva dribbling from his mustache—"She, poor little girl, is carrying two souls. She has to, because there's a soul that don't have no living body and got to use hers." He bends again and over her wails, blesses her in Gaelic (he tells me) and shambles on down the bleak Broadway sidewalk strewn with butts and torn paper, dog poop.

It is difficult to protect her from Manhattan's grim winter and the less-than-enlivening spring. A few trees, sparse green, no visible blossoms, and after a spring storm, a dead man lying at the foot of a statue of one of the university's presidents.

One day, I pack a lunch and wheel her to the nearby Hudson, to a bench beneath weeping willows. I nurse her and gaze at the river water full and lively after the night's rain; I compare it favorably to the Isar. While I am switching her to the other breast I notice her interest in something over my shoulder. There he is, a rat as big as a cat, leaning over the bench arm. She coos and holds out a hand. I jump from sitting, plunk her into the pram and run breathless back home.

I spend days, weeks, months gazing at her face, her feet, her able hands, her astonishing flesh, watching her lie on her stomach and turn the pages of a magazine. I know there's been a reprieve and I mutter my thanks, not to a God, for I don't believe, but superstitiously, just in case. I want the air of utterance to know that I am thankful every minute of each day.

When the heat of summer arrives, she and I fly west to stay with my parents. My husband follows reluctantly. He is behind in his promise to deliver a thesis. She turns one in August, and when she puts her bare feet on the grass at UC's Faculty Glade, she lets out an angry cry. She has never seen or touched grass and you can understand, can't you, that grass is frightening?

In the fall we move to Connecticut, where her father will be teaching boys, not girls, thought to be a wise move by both Barnard and Wesleyan. There are country walks, snow on the ground, an immense backyard, playmates on the cul-de-sac street. She is one, racing into two. She adores her father and each day tries to please him, with a hug, a picture she has drawn, a giggle when he tickles her, rapt listening when he sings a ballad. Her hair turns wavy, a reddish light brown.

In February, I am pregnant again and my diet declines steadily until all I am eating is soda crackers, drinking ginger ale. Soon I realize I don't *want* to cook dinner, type his papers, be a lover. My day is full without these tasks. Is there another woman somewhere who feels as I do? Billie Maguire, down the street, has a similar family—two children (one and three) and a husband teaching at Wesleyan. He takes long leaves to register voters in the South—Birmingham—and at night angry white citizens yell "Nigger-lover!" at her windows, throw rocks at her car. When we meet for lunch at my house, there is always a nervous edge to her; her hand trembles when she spoons sugar into her tea. Yet she never complains and if asked I'm certain she would have said she would like her life of duty towards husband to resume.

Our son arrives on his due date and sucks eagerly. There is lots of time to note and inspect his slightly mismatching ears, to kiss them and hug him closer when the gray fear threatens to envelop me. Ten fingers, ten toes, beautiful eyes, an early smiling mouth, why should ears match? One is elongated; the other has a small dip, or flop over. He is beautiful, everyone says that, and no one notices the ears. He is not a crosspatch. He smiles all the time he is awake; he never cries. My mother wonders if he is all right—shouldn't he cry? This question threatens to tip me a bit, but his smile is not that of a damaged child. He smiles approval of his world, his mother, his sister, milk, life. And his father, the sudden sight of him, sets him giggling, throwing his legs and arms around as though tetched.

I DON'T ASK AN INFORMED SCIENTIST if it's possible that *two* of my eggs were undamaged, were perhaps shielded by quantities of front-seat eggs, now lost in blood flow. I have an awareness of just how nutty such a question would seem. I would be trying to fasten down our knowledge of what was/is known, will be known, predictions of the future, summaries of the past, exactly what our esteemed scientists say they are trying to do.

Precious babies, sprung from our fragile loins, you walk, run, sing, dance, learn—you are on earth, you've escaped!

Knowing that my constant nuclear fear may seem dotty, I present excerpts from my RADIATION file, now oozing with news ignored by a majority of people here and abroad:

The New York Times, March 27, 2001
ILL URANIUM MINERS WAIT AS US
PAYMENTS LAPSE

The New York Times, June 8, 2001
US GOT BONES FROM AUSTRALIA
FOR A-TESTING
The cremated bones of Australian babies were shipped to the US and Britain from the 1950s to

the 70s without parental consent to test for radioactive fallout from nuclear tests, scientific documents show.

The New York Times, October 1, 2001
BRITISH USED BABIES' BONES IN TESTS
Parents of dead infants not told of a cold war atomic program.

USA Today, February 28, 2002
FALLOUT LIKELY CAUSED 15,000 DEATHS
Study links nuclear tests to cancer cases. Despite clamor, fallout study still unreleased. "No more stalling," one senator says. Local officials, citizen groups and researchers also want access.

THE ESTIMATED LAPSE OF TIME from exposure to "hot" environments and arrival of a carcinoma is twenty years. In 1966, on schedule, after living above the Radiation Lab in Berkeley, after working at Oak Ridge and Monsanto Chemical Company—contaminated environments—I undergo a radical mastectomy.

No chemo, no radiation, please, I say, I've had enough.

1966
VENTURA, CALIFORNIA

Do you want anything? Are you comfortable?"
Yes, my breast, and no, I'm not comfortable. Surely this nurse has something better to do. I'm sorry I'm morbid, sorry I don't like nurses or hospitals or doctors or comforting talk, sorry I display no interest in my wound, sorry I don't ask questions and allow her to refuse to answer, sorry I'm cancerous, bleeding, have a distant and numb left-dominant arm, and especially sorry I am not smiling through my tears. Sorry there are no tears. I want to behave well in all crises, and the least I could do is admit the nurse to my fear. But there is no fear, and even the idea of cri-

sis seems a bit much. I hurt and am reluctant to spread the news of pain.

"Do you have children?"

"Yes. Two. A boy and a girl."

"That's good. They'll need you to get well fast. Tomorrow or the next day we'll begin exercises that will help in your recovery."

I close my eyes. She's not pushy and I know she'll back off if I pretend sleep. I see a little breast wrapped in plastic, wedged beneath heavier garbage. I wonder again if it is whole or fragmented. If I could get up I might rescue it and stick it on with Elmer's Glue-All. If that doesn't work, perhaps a jar on the mantelpiece . . . a story I read about a miscarriage . . . the fetus beloved and preserved, indicating atmospheric change by its rise or fall in solution. My two breasts have felt wind, sun, water, desire and indifference. Rough and smooth hands have gently traced their surface, or grabbed and pulled. Milk has oozed out and infant noses have smelled the exit point beneath blouse or coat. My breasts have given direction when my head was yet puzzling meaning or consequence. Gut feeling is breast feeling and fear, pleasure, sorrow and shame begin in soft tissue, sink to stomach, or rise to neck, cheeks, ultimately pushing against semantic thickets. There is a main highway for love, from soft cone to a channel between my legs.

I cup my hand over my breast and feel a shape in my hand. I squeeze and it is as though the shape is attached to a stiff wall, at a distance from me, like a rotting peach caught on a fencepost nail. It is suffering . . . I've got to get it out of here . . . it misses its partner . . . don't be maudlin . . . it cannot live without . . . don't be morbid . . . don't cry . . . what good is crying? . . . be brave . . . I am sorry . . .

Women. How I dislike their confidences. Sometimes it seems they can only speak of loss, their ghettoed selves able only to talk of lands they can't visit. I listen through my walled silence while they speak to one another of what has been denied to them or taken away—love, breasts, babies, youth, figure, romance, security, peace of mind. They love to brag of heavy flow and crippling cramps, strange bladder symptoms, how many hours (or how few) they've been in labor, how many months of spastic colitis they've endured, the career they haven't followed, the piano they no longer have time for, the men they didn't marry, the miscarriages, how bad this year's flu has been, how often they are required to make love, have sex, do it, smear the diaphragm, how sick the children are, how little money there is and why it is his fault.

THERE IS NO PALLIATIVE (metaphor, myth, drug), no love deep enough to excise for more than a few hours a day my awareness of a missing breast. If this is bad news for others, I suggest they discard me. Here's the way to do it: Say I am neurotic, lack self-esteem, am morbid, self-centered, lack imagination. Say I should meditate. Say narcissim breeds desolation and misery. Soul is greater than its house. I should be glad I'm alive, should count my blessings. There. Easy, isn't it?

But beware. I shall mention the loss again and again, like all the women before me. Along with other unbalancing thoughts, it interests me. I'm like a three-legged dog. She can still run, but there's a difference in rhythm and in the feeling she evokes in the observer. She adjusts to tilt, but never, ever forgets the four-legged gait she used to have.

SUMMER 1991
NEVADA

I must *see* the invisible and conjure up signs of environmental damage from repeated aboveground bomb tests. Perhaps interview Nevada residents, collect anecdotal reports.

I drive my Honda northeast from San Francisco with my dog, Missy. Our first overnight is in a motel in Carson City, Nevada. She does not seem pleased. She doesn't bounce out of the car ready to explore as is her usual behavior. She enters our stuffy, furnished room slowly, does not check it out with her nose close to the floor, smelling previous occupants. When I say, "Just let me set up the typewriter and use the bathroom, and then we'll take a walk," she sighs and lies down with her face on her paws and her eyes on me. I feel her nose to see if she is sick, but no, her nose is cool. Her fur, usually fluffy, looks tired. I kneel on the carpet and fondle her soft ears, kiss her tufted eyebrows, bury my face in her ruff, but she pulls her head to one side and pushes my hands away with a paw. Perhaps she is hungry; that's what is wrong. I find her dish in the car, pour out her portion, run cool water over it from the rusty tap in the bathroom, and set it in front of her. She stands up, eats half and lies down again. Never before in my life with her has she refused food. "Missy," I say, "you are depressing me. Don't you know it's necessary for us to enjoy this trip? We are sisters on a journey and you're acting like a pouting child who has to be bribed until good mood is restored. I thought we didn't have to do that, you and I." No response at all, though she watches me, as usual.

I grab her leash and head for the door. Testing her, since she is still lying down, I say, "Well then, goodbye, see you later, I'm taking a walk." She gets up and follows me, but her tail is tucked in and she gives off a meaning far short of enthusiasm. She lags behind, sniffing tree trunks, lifting her leg to pee (she sometimes squats) until we reach a large park area that boasts scruffy grass and picnic tables. She likes to roll in grass but this grass is inferior. She is not giving me any indication of her joy in life, which I feed on. Sunset passes unnoticed and it is getting dark.

The park lights go on and there is no one around, no dogs to spark her interest, no children playing. Where is everybody? I sag down onto the ground with my back against the end of a picnic table, stretch my stiff legs, appreciate the absence of a mate for whom I'd have to look presentable at dinnertime. Missy lies down in front of me, stares at me. There is something eerie about how alone we are, woman and dog, as though the population has heard that a tornado is on its way and has taken cover. There is no wind, not even a slight breeze, and the leaves on the trees look as tired as Missy's fur. I play with the idea of a tornado, which I've never experienced, how interesting it might be to see tables fly, trees knocked to the ground, my arms around my dog, both of us thrown into the sky then hurled onto the earth. No ID found.

"Now then," I say to Missy (one ear up, then down again), "I have to decide whether you are depressed or sick. All your normal aspects of behavior are missing. Tail down, ears down, no energy, body not wiggling with interest in your surroundings, lagging behind instead of leading me on, not sitting up to listen to what I say, no interest in finishing your dinner. If I had dog ears and a dog tail and a dog athlete's body like yours and suddenly I didn't display them, I would hope my mistress would perceive that I was sad! Let's go find the car." As always, she performs this task at genius level, leads us back to the Honda and then into the motel room. I am exhausted and quickly get into bed. She puts a paw up on the side of the bed and utters a faint whine. She is, at home, allowed on the bed, in the bed. Why is she now hesitating and asking permission? I say "Up!" and soon I am wrapped around her, my fingers digging into her fur to inspect for ticks or rough places, my face buried in her neck ruff. Ah-h-h.

IN THE MORNING Missy and I head off on the sidewalk to look for a restaurant. I carry with me my yellow legal pad with the new Le Pen clipped to it. Missy leads and if not joyous, her tail is up and wagging. I need oatmeal, the one breakfast choice I'm sure can't be polluted, and many cups of coffee. I must study the *Nevada Handbook* and my AAA Triptik, if possible dilute my apprehension concerning Nevada. In my pantry at home I have fifty books about post-WWII radiation, and it occurred to me one day that the reason they are in a dark room closed off from the rest of the house is my fear that even *words* about radiation can maim and kill.

I settle myself at a table next to a window where I can see Missy lying on the sidewalk; she eyes me and I wave at her but she looks away, then pretends sleep. The coffee is instant but the oatmeal is freshly made, hot with a pat of butter melting and a plastic bottle of honey in place. I open the *Nevada Handbook* and turn quickly to an early section:

Environmental issues, page 19
This 1,350-square mile chunk of the Southern Nevada desert is a Rhode Island–sized area that's off limits—but you probably wouldn't want to go there even if it weren't. Between 1951 and 1962, 126 atmospheric tests of nuclear weapons were

conducted within the Test Site's boundaries. Between 1962 and 1992, another 925 underground explosions took place (that number was recently increased by 204 tests that the federal government conducted secretly).

I flip to one of the maps of Nevada to see if I'm in southern Nevada. I seem to be in western Nevada and shall soon be traveling through central Nevada, speeding towards Utah through the Great Basin Desert, which was named in 1844 by John Fremont. My handbook says:

> None of the rivers that flow into this desert ever flow out. Instead, they empty into lakes, disappear into sinks, or just peter out and evaporate. The Great Basin is not a basin at all. . . . Roughly 75% of Nevada is occupied by the Great Basin Desert. At the same time, roughly 75% of the Great Basin Desert is in Nevada.

I read that not only is this place not a basin, it contains "upwards of 200 discrete mountain ranges, between 50 and 100 miles long, separated by valleys of equal length." So, though those evil bits of radiation can easily cross a map line separating southern Nevada from central Nevada, they will have to penetrate mountains, sink into lakes, might even "peter out." The last item I read in my *Nevada Handbook* is a statement from a seventeen-year-old soldier who witnessed an above-ground explosion in 1957:

> That cloud was like a big ball of fire with black smoke and some red inside, big, monstrous, almost sickening. . . . It left me really sad, real apprehensive about life. . . . That explosion told me I was part of the most evil thing I have ever seen in my life.

I pay my bill, go back to my table to leave a generous tip, almost run outside to collect Missy. "Come on, let's go. We have a long drive ahead of us. Up! Up!" I tug on her leash and she looks at me, ears down as though she's done something wrong and hopes to be forgiven. I kneel down to stroke her soft ears. "No, sweetie, I'm not mad at you. I'm mad at Nevada, or at men who . . ." But that's not right. I'm afraid of something. I'm fighting tears in my throat and want to hurry away from them. Crying, that would be stupid, just like a woman, like me. "Come on, sad Missy, let's go find a mountain."

AAA guides me with a green Magic-Marker line to Highway 50, first to Fallon, Nevada, where I park next to a large grassy area in front of city hall, for Missy to roll on, and she does; I try to lure her into running with me but she scorns the invitation. Then on to New Pass Summit, an unbelievable six-thousand feet altitude. There's a pull-over look-at-the-view area and I see a car parked. A woman is standing beside her beige Volvo, her small dog on a leash. This is the first human being I've seen since Fallon and believing we have dogs in common, I walk slowly towards her. Missy does not greet her dog, and walks off into the brush, lifting her leg to pee, raising her nose to sniff. I say, "Nice view, isn't it?" She's about my age with coiffed hair; she's wearing a pale blue, well-pressed pantsuit. She leans down to pick up her dog, unlocks her car (I note that, locking and unlocking in this wilderness), gets in, fastens her seatbelt, revs quickly backward just past my feet, and drives off. I think ordinary thoughts—she's crazy, she's deaf, she's robbed a bank and is running from the law. Then I cloud over, my eyes mist. Almost blind, I step carefully into the high brush, trying to see Missy's plumed, white tail held high; there it is, the Real. The woman and her dog must have been an awake dream. Nonsense. I tell myself that woman just didn't like me.

At Austin, Nevada, we've driven 198 miles since breakfast and I'm hungry. When we began the climb to Austin, Missy stood up and put her nose out the window. We've been traveling at high altitudes much of the time and we both seem to feel invigorated, ready to take some exercise, see a few trails, smile at trees, congratulate the car for perfect behavior. I remember the guidebook said that Austin has fewer than three hundred residents, no doctor, no pharmacy, no barber shop, is at the geographical center of Nevada, has a typical Nevada attitude of tolerance for personal liberty. The town is antiqued by weather and no surface is level. All the buildings seem to have been built by weekend carpenters, the porches falling down, shacks containing stacked wood in backyards, dogs and cats indifferent to each other free to wander or sit in front yards. Silver and gold were mined here, but that was long ago. Melting snow is still making deep ruts beside the road. When I began this trip it was summer; here, it is spring and the streets are lined with white wisteria in bloom and yellow climbing roses, the scent heavy, the blossoms falling on the car, on the porches. Missy is pushing my shoulder with her paw, then turning around and around in the backseat, looking at a cat out one window, a dog through another.

I park beneath a fragrant wisteria and we start walking. Dogs, twelve of them, come running and all the tails are wagging. There's a daisy chain of rear-sniffing, but when I go on down the street Missy follows and the other dogs calmly sit down and watch us depart.

There's a dirt road and what looks like a trail leading up the slope. I turn to call Missy. She runs towards me, wearing her happy face. I know that sounds soggy but there is an expression of happiness that, in times past, has caused people to stop and say "What a happy dog!" stroke her head, say "Oh how soft!"; children hug her, kiss her back, want to take her home. I lean down, kiss her cool nose and say, "See, I told you a long ride was going to be fun."

My foot is out, ready to step onto the trail, Missy beside me, and there they are, two dead rabbits. Are they dead? They are lying so peacefully, no blood, and the one eye visible in the larger rabbit is open and un-clouded. My knees wobble as I crouch to get a closer look. I clutch Missy's collar to keep her back from them, and she points her paws in their direction, before lying down. She looks up at me and utters a faint whine. She's not interested in carrion unless it's gone rank and then she likes to roll in it. Of course I believe they've been shot. It's not natural for two rabbits to lie dead on a trail and what is not natural means guns, missiles, bombs, human mayhem. Fallout? I pick up a stick and slowly push it under the open-eyed bunny, turn him over, looking for the bullet hole, blood. He's stiff, very dead. No hole, no blood. I stand up, breathe deeply, look all around me at the mountain slopes, the tranquil town behind me, trying to smell danger. "Missy, do you still want to go up the trail?" She wags and wiggles and sets forth, tail high.

I follow her, feeding once more on her natural en-thusiasm, the curiosity that turns every walk into an adventure. I know she smells, sees, hears better than I can and on this trip I have wondered what information she's receiving that is not available to me, something making her gloom and droop. Movement through her paws from under the ground, distant blasts, the smell of ions and fear, iron cars rolling down tracks far under our surfaces? We climb steadily and I inhale, exhale, trying to instill a calm mind and a trust in my body. Now and then I pause to look across at the mountain to the south, which is already shadowed though it is just past noon, or to view the town of Austin, miniature, crowded in on itself, huddled, brave. Two church spires, the Minit Mart all-purpose store, the one main street called Main Street. I narrow my eyes and try to imagine snow covering the town, piled up around the churches, burying the cars, hiding the dogs and cats. Somewhere I read that even in summer the thermometer here can dip to below freezing, and there are crevices where it never thaws, where frozen animals do not decay; suicide in Austin would be easy in winter.

Missy is leaping and pouncing on imaginary critters in the brush. There's always a moment of stasis when she does this, her black/white body in the air, four feet above the ground, like a ballet dancer or a deer. I walk on, no longer hungry, watching my feet avoid ruts, pleased that my knees are strong, my ankles situated snugly in red-and-white Nikes.

I reach a point where the trail ends and I'm not brave enough to set off through sagebrush. I don't know what I'm afraid of but I haven't forgotten the rabbits. I call, "Missy, Missy, let's go back!" turn myself around and see three dead mice lying in the sun beside the trail. I yell, "MISSY! NOW!" and she bounds down the hill wearing her smile. I hunch over and stare at their ropy tails, closed eyes, the fur so glossy gray; Missy sniffs them and starts down the trail. I follow and talk while I look right and left off the rutted path into the brush, fearful that if I don't watch my feet I'll twist an ankle and be unable to reach the safety of my Honda, that I'll die from something lurking. "Missy." My voice is not loud but she hears and looks back at me. "Go on, keep going, I'll talk, we'll find the car and get out of here. You don't know about death, do you? You sniff it but you aren't equipped to fear it, anticipate it, worship it. Lucky you. You chase cats, rabbits, deer, gophers . . ." She stops on the trail, looks back at me, cocks her head, alert to those words of prey she knows. "No, keep walking. You've never caught anything, never killed, you just like to chase. As hunter, you're hopeless. You'd die in the wild. Long ago, you hitched yourself to humans, and I know I am your protector and there is danger here. I must get us back on the road, right?"

In the Minit Mart I buy peanuts and celery and toy with the question I'd like to ask the clerk, a confident young woman with a dark braid down her back. "Say, what's with the dead animals I keep seeing?" But everyone in the store is in slow motion, calm, dressed for a TV show about the Old West, shuffling on the broad, wooden floorboards, chatting, saying "Mighty nice weather, eh?" and I know she would say either "What dead animals?" or "What about them?"

Back inside the Honda, I check my AAA guide with its green line. I've not planned where we'll spend the night, how many miles ahead, how long we'll have to drive. Highway 50, Hickison Summit, then Pinto Summit (7,300 ft), town of Eureka, town of Ely, Connors Pass (7,700 ft) and on the next page, written in red Magic Marker—"No facilities available for 83 miles from Utah/Nevada border to Delta, Utah." Almost three hundred miles, but we've had some exercise and Missy is happy, let's go!

I drive with no thought of stopping, unwilling to ask Nevada residents about their fears, their history, their memories. I want to drive and drive, listen to country-western songs, speed through Utah, on to the Continental Divide in Colorado, too high an altitude for worry or thought.

2 0 0 2

MENDOCINO, CALIFORNIA

The last week in August 2002, I rent a house in
Mendocino, a house supposedly above the fog. I
take with me a suitcase of books about radiation and
a typewriter; I intend to finish this wavy-wandering
memoir of an adult life all too aware of hidden, un-
seen, unsmelled, unproven, lurking dangers denied so
often by those who claim knowledge. I once thought
my subject of nuclear dangers was compelling, even
somewhat interesting, though morbid. But then, one
year ago, nineteen strangers attacked Manhattan's towers and the Pentagon. And now my story suffers from
a lack of drama. My evildoers are only substantial scientists, trusted civil servants, national-security drones,

presidents, vice presidents, legislators, workers who perceive danger but have mortgages, families, children in college. These people do not interest me; I do not want to write about them. The nineteen . . . I try to deposit them in a section of hell reserved for the worst of our species, but they pop up again and again—dark, compelling, brave, composed and steady, internally flamboyant, fevered with plan, crazily drunk with Godness and belief, fueled by phosphorescent hatred. Their complicated deeds shimmer and glow, are sadly, memorably enormous, and—somehow—bewitchingly beautiful. Like everyone else, I shall see, as long as I am alive, the TV images of the towers slowly crumbling, the smoke chasing the fleeing spectators, the third tower swaying, then giving up, going down. And behind these images I see the mushroom cloud that has suddenly lost its power to shock. It is now relegated to the past and has found its level in the neighborhood of the Salem witch trials. I pluck at it, try to bring it back to sit with me in the house in Mendocino while I write, but its cloud now seems almost lacey, pretty, harmless.

I have always liked going off to a strange place, no

radio, no TV, for a limited stretch of time, to accomplish a well-defined writing task. The typewriter is out of its box, ready. I try to read the last book I'll need, a brute of a book by Dr. John Gofman, MD, PhD. Dr. Gofman spent his long life close to and employed in the science of the atomic age while at the same time questioning the safety of nuclear plants and weaponry. He is, and will remain, a rich source for the science needed to understand "health physics."

Idly turning pages, I find on page 740 "Section 2: The Stochastic in Utero Effects: Cancer and Leukemia Induction" (Goffman, *Radiation*). Suddenly I feel sleepy though it is morning and I've had two cups of coffee. I just haven't the steam to power me over "stochastic"—there is a dictionary on the shelf, but I know this word will not be in it. I don't *want* to know its meaning.

I step outside into the fog, and sucking in the damp air causes me to cry *again* because Missy is not with me, is in fact dead, a month gone, and once again I know that "with me" is just a manner of speaking. Of course she is with me in her absence, her excitement in a fog carrying me always forward, up the hill, following the creek bed, never losing sight of me, and

I needn't worry because she will always lead me home.
I blink and start down the road.

The house is surrounded by tall redwoods, and
some of their branch tips are brown. There is no other
house in sight, no human sound, not even the whine
of electric sawing. There is a cry nearby of a dog
locked inside an enclosure. Or a trap? A coyote? But
I've heard many coyotes and this is not a coyote yelp.
There is no voice of reproach or supplication. Later in
the day the cry will weaken and then stop. In the
evening the phone rings twice and there is someone
on the other end and then the click of hang up.

The next day dawns sunny, and I still steer away
from the typewriter. I read more Gofman: "There is a
strong tendency to forget how primitive medicine is
today in its appreciation of the problems caused by
low doses of radiation" (*Radiation,* 741). No, I haven't
read all those pages. My fingers and eyes have wan-
dered. I've read two novels and one book of short stories. I'm busy failing at my stated intention and
program. Each night, when my friend John calls, I say,
"Oh yes, I'm writing, writing. It's just great!"

The next morning, my third sunrise in this house

in Mendocino, I take my small bird-watcher binoculars outside and sit down on a bench with a view of the forest below and the surrounding trees. There is no wind, not a leaf moving. The house is ringed by bottlebrush and rosemary bushes, fuchsia in the shade, hydrangea in full bloom, rose trees, morning glory vines. I count the plants whose names I know and suddenly become aware of the source of my anxiety, the true source. It is not Missy's absence, though that is a part. Where are the birds? Where are the birds on the telephone line, in the trees, quivering the leaves? Where are the squirrels leaping from branch to branch, scampering across the clearing? Where are the bees on the columbine vine, the butterflies, the hummingbirds, the ants, potato bugs? The quail? And in the sky, where are the circling hawks so visible from my house in Mill Valley? And I've either gone abruptly totally deaf or there is indeed *no* sound sifting though the motionless redwood branches.

I get up and walk away from the bench onto the sere, tufted surface surrounding the house, and I notice for the first time that there are tire tracks indicating that a machine applied an herbicide around the house. I know fire is a constant worry here in this forest and yet . . . wait, I spot deer spoor, shiny, moist, and I plan to watch at sunset, which is the time when five deer visit the driveway of the house in Mill Valley.

I put out a pan of birdseed and a bowl of water, sit inside and watch. No takers. I grab my keys and drive to the Mendocino Little River beach and am so grateful to see the swarm of ducks, seagulls coming close for food scraps. They look a bit mussed but otherwise healthy.

On Wednesday morning I surrender and decide to return home the next morning. I have seen no deer. If they are here they know areas of danger and will not taste anything near this house. I resist the temptation to make a list of the reasons I am going home without accomplishing even a sentence. Though these words are in the present tense, that is artifice. They were written three days after my safe return to the land of raucous crows, twenty-eight quail trailing each other across my grass, squirrels chewing on pinecones high in the trees above the driveway then throwing the stripped cone at my car (or me), deer peering through my gate, hoping, or just interested.

It is clear to me the nineteen aliens have a much better story, one that does not require twenty years to mature, to reveal its nature. They have provided instant death, multiple ministories, countless funerals, many hundreds of father- or motherless children. No one has to sit at a typewriter and try to prove something. They have even succeeded in controlling how we think about their after-death lives, the seven (seventeen? seventy?) virgins sitting at their feet, listening to the tales of deafening triumph.

The Havahart cage—"caring control of small animals"—is one of those inventions, like atomic reactors, that seeks to assure us that we are a kind, considerate, innovative, lifesaving species. We may arrange to kill five million red-wing blackbirds because they are eating our corn, but we have an enclosure, a trap, that can catch a skunk (or a porcupine, a squirrel, a rat, a cat, a small dog, a possum, a raccoon) so that we do not have to shoot it, poison it, glue its legs to a sticky surface, or chop it into two bloody pieces.

I have a long experience with Havahart cages; I've evolved in compassion as the cage has been marketed first locally, then throughout California, and eventually nationwide. Apparently many customers want to be kind to the animals that are driving them crazy. Picture me, in Santa Cruz, twenty years ago. I am trying hard to produce a lovely garden. I can stand in my kitchen and watch darling, little brown rabbits eat my snapdragons, my geraniums, my pansies, down to the brown earth, and when I open the door, they scamper away. I buy my first (and last) gun, a BB gun. I plan merely to scare them. One day my twenty-year-old daughter picks up the gun outdoors, aims, fires, and a rabbit falls over dead. She throws down the gun and cries. She says, "Mom, why did you let me do that? Throw that thing, that awful gun AWAY!" So I do, without ever learning how to take aim.

After that, I buy my first Havahart cage. I study the directions, put peanut butter on the bait pan, set the trigger, and place the cage on the deck outside my studio. The next morning there is a little, scared rabbit cringing inside and my coydog (coyote and shepherd mix) is frenzied, panting, batting at the sides, trying to poke a paw in through the strong aluminum crosspieces. No, I am not going to let the dog devour the bunny, so I put the cage in the trunk of the car, the dog in the backseat, and we drive to a wooded area nearby. I give the rabbit a head start and then let the dog go in pursuit. In a few minutes she returns, and no blood is dripping from her mouth.

I am pleased with this easy way of dispatching rabbits, but more and more of them dine on my flowers. They can devour faster than I can set the trap.

So, one day I catch a rabbit, call the dog to my side, open the cage, and let the dog sink her teeth into the neck of the frightened bunny. She does not eat her prey. Too easy, perhaps.

One evening, at sunset, I look out the window and see a raccoon standing in the garden with the cage in his arms, a rabbit inside. Soon after that I give up and begin admiring the profusion of weeds that take over. I often hear gunshots and know that my neighbors are not as resigned as I am. Hawks take care of the smaller animals.

My present Havahart is more complicated. It has two entrances and thus is more difficult to set. I buy it after encountering a skunk. It did not spray me, but the next night it sprayed Missy and we suffered for days. I place the cage again and again at the bottom of the yard and each morning the bait is gone, the doors slammed shut, but no animal inside. Finally, one skunk is removed by the Humane Society, which informs me that while they can kill the animal, I am not allowed to, thank goodness.

I continue to set the trap to catch relatives of the skunk. Each morning—sometimes the bait is gone but the trap has not sprung, sometimes, when I go to put the bait on the dish, the dish is gone. Often the trap is sprung, bait gone, no animal inside. I can't figure out how they can eat the bait, spring the trap, and avoid getting caught by the slamming doors. I keep on setting, looking, wondering.

My compassion level is rising, but I am beginning to lack faith in the invention or the cleverness of the manufacturers. One morning, expecting to find yet another empty, sprung cage, I bend to lift the cage and it seems heavy. I back away and peer close, and, yes, there is something brownish and furry inside—but no white, so probably, one would hope, not a skunk. Wary of drawing too near, though, I hook a rake over one of the crosspieces and drag the cage up to the front gate of the garden. In the sunlight I can see it is an ugly possum. I know a possum on sight because once in Hollywood at a nursery school where I was substituting, a possum got into the playhouse and wouldn't come out. We had to keep all the children inside while the fire department rescued the animal and all the children cheered. This possum I have in my cage, when I turn my back on him to open the gate, vanishes. Just like that. The doors are still down, no exit possible. But gone he is.

A few days pass. I set the cage again. The next morning I find a sprung trap and an animal caught, half of its body inside, half outside through the square space between the cross rods, stuck. The doors are down. Its face has been chewed off in the night, blood on the leaves below the cage. I close my eyes and grab it around its headless neck and pull. It comes clear and I see the long ropy tail belonging to a very large rat. My glove is streaked with blood. I wrap the body in a newspaper and throw it into the creek below the house. My glove goes into the garbage can. I hose down the cage.

It is early September; the leaves are falling, and the skyscrapers.

People are jumping from the highest floors, their stick-figure legs and arms spread wide.

I see the towers crumple again and again on TV, and someone says their children think it happens many times.

I try to remember nuclear fear. Substitute terrorist fear.

I am glad I won't be living much longer.

Let Skye and Lacey, my grandchildren, grow steadily into this world now grown so small.

Let them tilt their heads to watch the circling, floating hawks; let them look closely at inchworms and sense the life hidden inside their fragile green and tan bodies.

See how the hawks dive for prey and the inchworms measure their route, and at the end of the twig I hold in my hand; they swiftly turn around and go back on their tightrope, searching for the leaves they need to survive.

SELECTED BIBLIOGRAPHY

Many books, articles, even movies, have been produced on the general subject of nuclear health and low-dose radiation. Listed below are books that have been on my shelf for many years. Others are more recent, more urgent. I have read the books, or looked through their pages, again and again, to help me focus, or to widen my search for evidence, or simply to immerse again in fret and worry, leading me once again to the typewriter.

Bartimus, Tad, and Scott McCartney. *Trinity's Children: Living Along America's Nuclear Highway.* New York: Harcourt Brace Jovanovich, 1991.

Brown, Michael. *Laying Waste: The Poisoning of America by Toxic Chemicals.* New York: Pocket Books, 1981.

Caldicott, Helen. *Missile Envy: The Arms Race and Nuclear War.* New York: Bantam Books, 1986.

Cooper, Helen M., ed. *Arms and the Woman.* Chapel Hill: University of North Carolina Press, 1989.

Elshtain, Jean Bethke. *Women and War.* New York: Basic Books, 1987.

Emerson, Gloria. *Winners and Losers.* New York: W. W. Norton, 1985.

Enloe, Cynthia. *Bananas, Beaches and Bases.* Berkeley: University of California Press, 1990.

Fisher, Phyllis K. *Los Alamos Experience.* Japan Publications, 1985.

Ford, Daniel. *Meltdown: The Secret Papers of the Atomic Energy Commission.* New York: Simon & Schuster, 1986.

Fradkin, Philip L. *Fallout: An American Nuclear Tragedy.* Phoenix: University of Arizona Press, 1989.

Fuller, John G. *The Poison that Fell from the Sky.* New York: Berkley Books, 1997.

———. *We Almost Lost Detroit.* New York: Ballantine Books, 1975.

Gale, Robert Peter, and Thomas Hauser. *Final Warning: The Legacy of Chernobyl.* New York: Warner Books, 1988.

Gofman, John W. *An Irreverent, Illustrated View of Nuclear Power.* Committee for Nuclear Responsibility.

———. *Radiation-Induced Cancer from Low-Dose Exposure.* Committee for Nuclear Responsibility, 1990.

Gofman, John W., and Arthur R. Tamplin. *Poisoned Power.* Emmaus, PA: Rodale Press, 1979.

Griffin, Susan A. *A Chorus of Stones: The Private Life of War.* New York: Doubleday, 1992.

Hacker, Barton C. *Elements of Controversy: The Atomic Energy Commission and Radiation Safety in Nuclear Weapons Testing, 1947–1974.* Berkeley, University of California Press, 1981.

Heilbron, J. L., and Robert W. Seidel. *Lawrence and His Laboratory.* Berkeley: University of California Press, 1989.

Herken, Gregg. *The Winning Weapon: The Atomic Bomb in the Cold War.* Princeton: Princeton University Press, 1981.

London Observer Correspondents. *Chernobyl: The End of the Nuclear Dream.* New York: Vintage, 1987.

May, John. *The Greenpeace Book of the Nuclear Age.* New York: Pantheon, 1989.

Morgan, Karl Z., and Ken M. Peterson. *The Angry Genie: One Man's Walk through the Nuclear Age.* Norman: University of Oklahoma Press, 1999.

O'Connell, Robert L. *Of Arms and Men: A History of War, Weapons and Aggression.* New York: Oxford University Press, 1989.

Pringle, Peter, and James Spigelman. *The Nuclear Barons.* New York: Avon, 1981.

Rhodes, Richard. *The Making of the Atomic Bomb.* New York: Simon & Schuster, 1988.

Stewart, George R. *The Year of the Oath: The Fight for Academic Freedom of the University of California.* Garden City: Doubleday, 1950.

Tredici, Robert Del. *At Work in the Fields of the Bomb.* New York: Harper & Row, 1987.

Weart, Spencer. *Nuclear Fear: A History of Images.* Cambridge, MA: Harvard University Press, 1988.

Welsome, Eileen. *The Plutonium Files: America's Secret Medical Experiments in the Cold War.* New York: Dial Press, 1999.

Wilson, Jane S., and Charlotte Serber, eds. *Standing By and Making Do: Women of Wartime Los Alamos.* Los Alamos Historical Society, 1988.

Wyden, Peter. *Day One: Before Hiroshima and After.* New York: Simon & Schuster, 1984.